CAMPAIGN 269

ALESIA 52 BC

The final struggle for Gaul

NIC FIELDS

ILLUSTRATED BY PETER DENNIS

Series editor Marcus Cowper

First published in Great Britain in 2014 by Osprey Publishing,

PO Box 883, Oxford, OX1 9PL, UK
PO Box 3985, New York, NY 10185-3985, USA
E-mail: info@ospreypublishing.com

ISBN: 978 1 78200 922 1
E-book ISBN: 978 1 78200 924 5
E-pub ISBN: 978 1 78200 923 8

Editorial by Ilios Publishing Ltd, Oxford, UK (www.iliospublishing.com)
Index by Zoe Ross
Typeset in Myriad Pro and Sabon
Maps by Bounford.com
3D bird's-eye view by Donato Spedaliere
Battlescene illustrations by Peter Dennis
Originated by PDQ Media, Bungay, UK
Printed in China through Worldprint Ltd.

14 15 16 17 18   10 9 8 7 6 5 4 3 2 1

ARTIST'S NOTE

Readers may care to note that the original paintings from which the colour plates in this book were prepared are available for private sale. The Publishers retain all reproduction copyright whatsoever. All enquiries should be addressed to:

Peter Dennis, Fieldhead, The Park, Mansfield, Notts, NG18 2TT, UK
magie.h@ntlworld.com

The Publishers regret that they can enter into no correspondence upon this matter.

THE WOODLAND TRUST

Osprey Publishing are supporting the Woodland Trust, the UK's leading woodland conservation charity, by funding the dedication of trees.

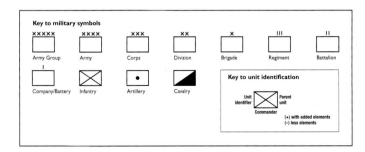

CONTENTS

The Roman Empire at the time of Caesar's first consulship

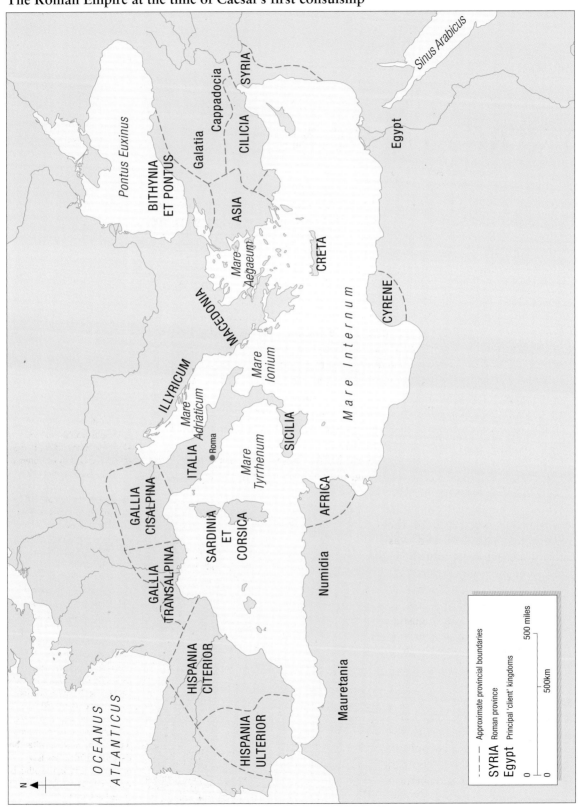

INTRODUCTION

The desire by political and military leaders to be known to the generations to come and, naturally, to cast him or herself in a good light, is no recent phenomenon. Such memoirs are by nature subjective and complete adherence to the truth should not be expected, especially if the author had written memoranda with at least one eye on the future record.

Caius Iulius Caesar himself took unusual – though by no means entirely unprecedented – steps to ensure that his own approved version of events was the one that was most widely and authoritatively disseminated. An adroit and conscious user of propaganda, both at home and abroad, his *commentarii* on his campaigns in Gaul, what was properly known as the *Commentarii de Bello Gallico*, are not the work of a man of letters but of a man of action who narrates events in which he has himself played the leading part. In a society where personal glory mattered so much and military proficiency was the sine qua non of the ruling elite, this was an appropriate thing to do. Yet the manipulation of a narrative to show oneself in the best possible light may appear to a modern reader to be duplicitous.

For those who wish to be more charitable to Caesar, his work is what it is; it does not pretend to be another thing. On the other hand, the learned and accomplished Asinius Pollio believed that Caesar 'did not always check the truth of the reports that came in, and was either disingenuous or forgetful in describing his own actions' (*DI* 56.4). Asinius Pollio, who survived the civil wars of 49–31 BC to write a history of Rome under Augustus, may indeed have had a point. For it is possible to convict Caesar of both *suppressio veri*, suppression of the truth, and *suggestio falsi*, suggestion of what was untrue. There is much to be said, indeed, for looking at Caesar in the cultural context of the period. According to a credible report in Suetonius, upon the termination of his command in Gaul, Caesar

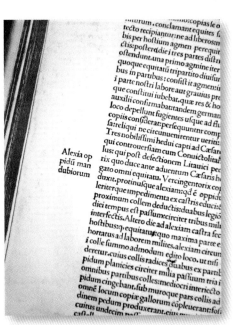

Liber Septimus (MuséoParc Alésia), from the library of the Guicciardini family of Florence – the seventh *commentarius* written by Caesar (*BG* 7.68.1). Caesar was not just one of the most prominent men at Alesia, he was also the author of the only eyewitness account we have of the siege. The elements of power at Rome, as taught by Sulla and confirmed by Pompey, were three: wealth, patronage and – not least – the loyalty of veteran legions (through which soldiers hoped to secure provision of land grants for them on demobilization). Caesar can be said to have added a fourth, namely 'be the author of your own events'. As a good, clear writer, he was skilled in public relations. Still, there are two methods by which a writer can deceive a reader. One is by relating false facts; the other is by manipulating true ones. (© Esther Carré)

dwelt on his position as *princeps civitatis*, leading citizen: 'It is harder to push me down from first place to second than from second to last' (*DI* 29.1). It mattered, who was first and who was second.

Certainly the most successful Roman commander of any period, Caesar was also a gifted writer. 'Avoid an unfamiliar word', he used to say, 'as a sailor avoids the rocks' (Aulus Gellius *Noctes Atticae* 1.10.4). Of all his surviving work, which was apparently voluminous (*DI* 56), Caesar's *commentarii* on his Gallic campaigns remain the best known and the most frequently referred to, and it is the work that has gripped most readers (and infuriated some). The writing style in the *commentarii* is that of a detailed factual report, prepared year by year, of the events as they unfold. They are elegantly written. Caesar wrote seven of the eight, the last being added, shortly after Caesar's death, by his friend Aulus Hirtius, who had served with him. As the French statesman and essayist Michel de Montaigne (1533–92) complained, 'the only thing to be said against him is that he speaks too sparingly of himself' (*Essais* 2.10, 'Des livres'). Caesar certainly chooses to ignore the triumvirate and its renewal at the Luca conference in the spring of 56 BC, and he does not give us his own account of the final deterioration of relations between himself and Pompey. On the other hand, Caesar would have his readers believe that his purpose was to bring stability to Gaul. However, he fails to explain why the Gauls repeatedly rebelled against his rule, even being willing to invite aid from the far side of the Rhine, and why his Aedui and Remi allies continued to intercede with him on the behalf of defeated rebels. Worse, he masks the war's horrendous cost in human life and suffering. This is not to say that Caesar blatantly falsifies events. In his adopted role of the omniscient *auditor ab extra* (viz. seeing everything), his techniques were omission, shift of emphasis (conscious or unconscious), and additions of his own observations.

To the Gauls in their homeland, Rome, in the guise of Caesar, was probably the worst enemy they ever had. Still, the conquest was no walkover. Hindsight is easy, and to us wise after the event, Caesar's selective presentation of the situation suggests that Gaul appeared to have been temporarily subdued rather than permanently mastered. This is nowhere more clear than in the case of the greatest revolt of all, which began as the year 53 BC drew to a close. After almost six years in Gaul, the Roman occupation was in a perilous condition. Caesar's continued strategy of annihilation had engendered a spirit of desperation, which detonated into an armed rebellion of Gaulish tribes under the leadership of a charismatic young noble of the Arverni, the powerful tribe who inhabited the region west of Mons Cevenna (Cévennes). He was called Vercingetorix.

Vercingetorix was adamant in his conviction that Gaul's only safety lay in a pan-Gaulish coalition, and in the year that lay ahead the Gauls were to make common cause against Caesar, in the course of which he was to learn that Gaulish fighting could be a very serious business and threaten not only his conquests but the reputation on which his political survival depended. Roman destructive brutalities were a convincing recruiting sergeant, and literally dozens of tribes swore allegiance to the young Vercingetorix, including many Caesar had thought were securely loyal. Though the Gaulish peoples shared a common language and culture, forging a fighting coalition amongst a mosaic of fiercely independent tribes all demonstrating an innate genius for creating chaos was a virtually impossible feat, and it was a tribute to Vercingetorix's personality and skill.

A CLASH OF CULTURES

The civilizing influence of classical culture has pretty much coloured our view of peoples beyond the frontiers of the Graeco-Roman world, the usual stereotype of them as 'different from us'. Greek commentators tended to perpetuate the idea of a coherent 'nation' identity, as can be witnessed in passing references to the Celts in the works of Herodotos, Xenophon, Plato and Aristotle. These earlier writers give a somewhat romantic picture of the Celts with a greater stress on such aspects as single combat and the wearing of torques, the latter adornment being the attribute *par excellence* of the Celtic warrior. On the other hand Roman commentators, such as Caesar and Tacitus, are more matter of fact, though Caesar's presentations of his enemies are subtly contrived to reflect his own glory.

'The Dying Gaul' (Rome, Musei Capitolini, inv. MC 747), usually thought to be a later Roman copy of the 2nd-century Pergamene original. Graeco-Roman art regularly depicted Gauls being defeated in battle or, as in this case, spilling their lifeblood on the field of defeat. Initially, the Romans were terrified by these imposing warriors, who adorned themselves with torques and wore hair that was slaked with lime to make it stand up like a horse's mane. Though the Greeks and Romans had heard of the Gauls, they first encountered them as warriors. It was in battle that their enormous size and outlandish appearance first struck them, usually with terror. By the time of the Gallic campaigns, Romans and Gauls had been battling against each other on and off for more than three centuries. Even Caesar occasionally betrays a sneaking admiration for the way they fought in his *commentarii*. (© Nic Fields)

'Le guerrier de Vachères' (Avignon, Musée Calvet, inv. G 136c), found c.1865 at Vachères (*département* of Alpes-de-Haute-Provence), and dated to the 1st century BC. This limestone statue, which would have stood around 2m tall (it survives to 1.53m), shows the characteristic iron mail-shirt, long-sleeved tunic, heavy woollen cloak, tubular torque and sword-belt of the aristocratic Gaulish warrior. Just visible under the cloak is the shoulder doubling, which serves as extra protection against downward blade strokes. A long slashing sword, for all to see, hangs at his right hip, and he leans on his body shield (oval or hexagonal) in characteristic Gaulish fashion. What may be a surprise is the fact the warrior is depicted clean-shaven and with short hair. Still, the scowling barbarian with long locks and matted beard is a stock figure on Roman triumphal monuments. (© Nic Fields)

Who the Celts were, and indeed if they ever existed as a recognizable ethnic entity, is a lively topic of scholarly debate, particularly among archaeologists. For our purposes 'Celt' was a general-purpose name applied by these Graeco-Roman writers (*Keltai* and *Galatai* by the Greeks, *Celtae*, *Galli* and *Galatae* by the Romans) to a population group occupying lands mainly north of the Mediterranean region from Galicia in the west to Galatia in the east. Though the notion that there was such a thing as a pan-Celtic Europe, a kind of brotherhood of the Celts, is the confection of nationalist politicians and popular writers, Celtic unity is recognizable by common speech and common artistic traditions.

It is generally accepted that the primary elements of Celtic culture originated with the Late Bronze Age Urnfield people (named for their large-scale cremation-burial in flat cemeteries) of the upper Danube basin, commencing circa 1300 BC and roughly coincident with the decline of Mycenaean power, who probably spoke a proto-Celtic language. By about 700 BC bronze working was gradually overtaken by iron working, and as a result the Urnfield culture was transformed into the Early Iron Age culture known as Hallstatt (after the type-site in the Salzkammergut massif of the Hallein/Salzburg area of Upper Austria). It may have been the availability of iron weapons that allowed and encouraged cultures that we may term Celtic to appear in the Iberian Peninsula and the British Isles as early as the 8th and early 7th centuries BC. Roman writers gave various reasons for these migrations – overpopulation, a search for a better climate or, as they were warriors, a delight in war and booty. There might be an element of truth in all or some of these reasons, but we should not take the elder Pliny seriously when he says (*HN* 12.2.5, cf. DS 5.26.3) the Gauls were so enthralled by the novel Bacchante pleasures of wine drinking that they seized their arms, took their families, and set off poste haste to pour over the Alps onto the wealthy plains of Italy.

Wine lovers or not, Celtic culture continued unabated with the emergence of a highly innovative Late Iron Age culture known as La Tène (after the type-site of La Tène near Lac Neuchâtel in Switzerland) in about 500 BC. This new culture was so strong that it gave Gaulish warriors the power to break through the defences of the classical world and reach the Mediterranean: Rome sacked in 390 BC; Delphi devastated in 279 BC; central Anatolia conquered in 277 BC. The Mediterranean world may have known and feared them as fierce fighters and superb horsemen, yet the Gauls' political sense was weak, and they were crushed between the migratory Germans and the power of Rome, to be ejected by the former, and conquered outright by the latter.

You cannot divorce geography from history, yet it is not only landscapes that matter, but also the peoples who inhabit them. Caesar famously opens his first *commentarius* with a brief description of what he identifies as Gaul, dividing its inhabitants, culturally and linguistically, into three broad groups, the Celtae or Galli, the Aquitani, and the Belgae. Caesar goes on to give some geographical precision to these divisions. The first group were located in the centre between the Garunna (Garonne) and Sequana (Seine), the second in Aquitania (Aquitaine) south-west of the Garunna, and the third north-east of the Sequana and Matrona (Marne). Of the three, Caesar held that the Belgae were the most courageous. The numerous and widespread Belgic peoples were

still largely untouched, as Caesar says, by the enervating luxuries of Mediterranean life, and they were probably mixed with Germanic peoples from east of the Rhenus (Rhine).

His fellow Romans would have referred to these regions collectively as Gallia Comata (Long-haired Gaul). A fourth region is usually referred to by Caesar as Provincia, the Province. Its official name was Gallia Transalpina (Gaul-across-the-Alps) in contrast to Gallia Cisalpina (Gaul-this-side-of-the-Alps). In the Italian peninsula the Rubicon (Rubicone) marked the boundary between Gallia Cisalpina and Italy proper. Gallia Transalpina, unlike Gallia Comata, was already part of the empire. It had been under Roman domination, if not a fully organised province, for three-quarters of a century, following the development of Roman links with the Greek trading colony of Massalia (Roman Massilia, whence Marseille), and the establishment of a permanent fortified outpost at Aquae Sextiae (Aix-en-Provence), the site of Caius Marius' victory against the Teutones in 102 BC. Gallia Transalpina gave the Romans a vital land route from north Italy to Iberia, where Roman influence had been much longer established. The control of this land route, along which successive Roman armies passed, and the safeguards of Roman economic interests were therefore a major concern to the Senate. Cicero could claim in the *pro Fonteio* that 'all Gaul is filled with Italian traders (*negotiatores*), all Provincia is full of Roman citizens' (11), and beneath the rhetoric there is solid truth. So when the stability of Gaul was threatened by the migration *en masse* to the west of one of the Celtic tribes of what is now Switzerland, the Helvetii, and the political machinations of the Germanic war leader Ariovistus, Caesar was provided with an admirable excuse to march his legions deep into unchartered territory.

Detail from a full-scale replica (Saint-Germain-en-Laye, Musée d'archéologie nationale) of the Gundestrup Cauldron (Copenhagen, Nationalmuseet), discovered by peat cutters at Gundestrup, Jutland (1891). Dismantled and deposited in a peat bog, presumably as a votive offering, the gilded silver cauldron was likely made in the Balkans sometime during the late 2nd century BC. Seen here is one of the seven interior plates (Plate E), showing in the upper register a procession of horse warriors, who provided the highest quality troops in any Celtic army. They were drawn chiefly from the nobles – the *equites* mentioned by Caesar in his *commentarii*. In the lower register there is a procession of armed warriors, the last of which wears a helmet with a crest in the form of a wild boar (a chieftain, perhaps), while at the end are three warriors blowing *carnyxes*, Celtic war trumpets. (© Esther Carré)

As was often the case in Rome's history, it was a clash of alien cultures that could only meet in war. A new model army led by Caesar's uncle had saved Italy from the threatened invasion of the Teutones and the Cimbri (102 BC, 101 BC), whose victories inflicted on earlier Roman commanders echo ominously in the background of the *commentarii*. The vivid memory of the near disaster remained, however, and served as a frightening reminder to Rome that a new northern barbarian threat could suddenly emerge at any time. Barbarian migrations were the stuff of Roman nightmares, and Caesar made good use of it by playing up the 'Germanic menace' in his writings. More to the point, he also had the wit to revive fears of the Gauls that dated from the sack of Rome (390 BC), and advertised them as a race without civilization who were not above burning alive their prisoners of war.

Compared to the Germanic world, seething with turbulence and turmoil, Gaul looked like a rich prize or prey. Thus Caesar's assessment of the Gaulish political scene – Gaul would have to become Roman or it would be overrun by the fierce warlike race from across the Rhine – was a nice tale, plausibly told. In all likelihood, it was a gross hyperbole but as a justification for his Gallic campaigns it would have convinced many who remembered the panic of fifty years before. It should not be forgotten that generals aim to win their reputations by offensives. Doubtless we should also make allowance for Caesar's desire for glory and booty, which would improve his position in the intense struggle for power that then dominated the political arena back home. The battle for Gaul Caesar certainly regarded as his own. The pickings would be rich, or so it was hoped, and excuses were easy to find. Military ambitions for a glorious conquest did the rest.

For both Caesar and the audience for whom he wrote, the Rhine marked the boundary between the known and the unknown. But to envisage it as the boundary between the Gaulish and the Germanic tribes was little more than a simplistic concept of a natural frontier, which stemmed from the fact that the world of the writer and his audience had very little to do with the Rhine – their centre was Rome. Likewise, Caesar's tripartite division of the inhabitants of Gaul was an oversimplification. It is evident from recent archaeological studies of settlements in what was northern Gaul that some of the tribes known as Germanic to Roman aristocrats may well have been what we now call La Tène Celtic, or a mixture of the two. Obviously the cultural boundary between Celt and German had not been such a sharp edge, defined by the Rhine, but a broad and vague band of hybridisation that extended on both sides of the river. What was politically conceived as a clear geographical dividing line was persistently diffused by the ebb and flow of history. Indeed, it seems that the territory between the Seine and the Rhine shared a cultural gradient between Celtic and Germanic that was constantly being reformed by migration and conquest, the latter expressing the political mobility of power but not necessarily of whole populations.

In fact, Caesar contradicts his own assertion that the Rhine was a natural frontier on a number of occasions. The Belgae, who lived south of the Rhine in northern Gaul, 'were of German extraction' says Caesar (*BG* 2.4.1), while the Menapii, another Belgic tribe, had their settlements 'on either side of the river' (*BG* 4.4.2). Similarly, he imparts that the Volcae Tectosages were a Gaulish people living beyond the Rhine (*BG* 6.224.2). Nonetheless, the overall description of Gaul that he offers is at best a generalization. The population of Gaul – as of the Celtic territories generally – were descended both from earlier

Caesars's Gallic campaigns 58–51 BC

CORNOVII

CORITANI

ORDOVICES

DEMETAE

BRITANNIA

ICENI

SILURES

DOBUNNI   CATUVELLAUNI

ATREBATES   TRINOVANTES   ● Camulodunium   **55**

BELGAE   ● Londinium

DUROTRIGES   REGNENSES   **54**   CANTIACI

DUMNONII

Oceanus Britannicus

Oceanus Germanicus

GERMANIA

Rhenus f.

MENAPII   **55**

MORINI   MENAPII   EBURONES   CUGERNI

NERVII   **54**   ATUATUCI

Nemetacum ●   ● Atuatuca   CAEROSI   **55**

AMBIANI   ATREBATES   ● Bagacum   CONDRUSI   **53**

CALETI   ● Samarobriva   SEGNI   TREVERI

VENELLI   BELLOVACI   VIROMANDUI   TREVERI

BOIOCASSES   VELIOCASSES   SUESSIONES   MEDIOMATRICI

56 ←   *Sequana f.*   PARISII   REMI   ● Divodurum

EBUROVICES   ● Lutetia   CATUVELLAUNI   LEUCI

CORIOSOLITES   REDONES   DIABLINTES   SENONES   TRICASSES   LINGONES   LATOVICI

OSISMII   CENOMANI   Autricum ●   ● Agedincum   ● Andematunnum

VENETI   ● Suindinum   **52**

NAMNETES   CARNUTES   ● Cenabum   Alesia ●   **58**

56   ANDECAVI   TURONES   **52**   MANDUBII   RAURICI   HELVETII

Liger f.   Noviodunum ●   ● Vesontio

BITURIGES   ● Avaricum   Bibracte ●   SEQUANI

● Limonum   **52**   ● Gorgobina   **58**

CUBI   ARVERNI   AEDUII

PICTONES   ARVERNI   AMBARRI   **58**

LEMOVICES   SEGUSIAVI   ● Genava

SANTONI   **52** Gergovia ●   Lugdunum ●

Oceanus Atlanticus   CADURCI   VELLAVI   ● Vienna

● Burdigala   PETROCORII   **51**

BITURICES   ● Uxellodunum   ● Ocelum   ● Taurasia

NITIOBROGES   GABALI

CADURCI   ● Genua

Garumna f.   RUTENI

56

Tolosa ●   VOLCAE   VOLCAE   ● Arelate

TECTOSAGES   ARECOMICI   SALLUVII   ● Aquae Sextiae   ● Nicea

Carcaso ●   ● Massilia   COMMONI

SORDONES   ● Narbo Martius

BEBRYCES

HISPANIA

Iberus f.

Mare Ligusticum

N

● Prinicipal *oppidum*

COMMONI   Celtic tribes

←   Caesar's Gallic campaigns, 58–51 BC

0 ———————— 200 miles

0 ———————— 200km

peoples and from the Celts (and others) who had migrated there. Furthermore, the Gauls were not a nation; in Gaul there would have been a complex web of interdependency and domination between tribes, which themselves were at different stages of social development. In the main these tribes, great and small, lived in proto-towns that Caesar applied the term *oppida*. They were typically sprawling agglomerations of buildings and enclosures, both private and public, with streets and elaborate defences. But the *oppida* were not chaotic, being organized in an organic rather than planned fashioned. Some were situated on hilltops, but many were in valley locations. The Gaulish *oppida* imply the existence of urbanized societies that could produce and organize food surpluses, in addition to whatever political implications they may have had.

Urbanized or not, for most Romans the 'barbarians' *par excellence*, the quintessential 'other', were the Gauls, who were seen as continual threat to Rome. With the tribal, clan and family structure at the focus of its social organisation, Gaulish society was often characterized as 'heroic', dominated by the warrior ethic. Along with this view of a different and threatening culture went ideas of hostility. Historically among the most feared enemies of Rome, the Gauls fought in an undisciplined manner, heedlessly rushing into contact swinging long swords. The Romans had traditionally found these wild, tall (by comparison) temperate zone warriors terrifying, and Graeco-Roman observers tended to see them at best as beguiling 'noble savages' (in truth, a Stoic exaggeration to scold Roman decadence), at worst as backward, wayward and dangerous. The Gauls, however, have left no written record themselves, at least in part because of their custom of oral transmission of law, tradition and religious practices. Even though archaeology is but a partial replacement, current archaeological discoveries are at least helping to correct this rather distorted view.

Gaulish society embraced several social orders. In the upper tier was the tribal nobility from whom the rulers would be drawn as well as the leaders of warrior bands, seers and bards. In the next group were the warrior farmers and craftsmen, and below them the serfs and slaves. Unlike contemporary Germanic society, however, Gaulish society possessed many of the institutions of the early state, a number of tribes having already abandoned hereditary kingship and instead having annually elected magistrates and popular assemblies of free adult males – Caesar singles out for mention the Arverni, the Aedui, and the Helvetii. On the other hand, as among the Germans, the nobles' prestige was measured in the size of retinues, for nobles displayed their status by the number and the fame of the warriors who lived at their expense under an obligation to fight for them. Added to these were the nobles' dependants or clients, the freemen attached to them in a somewhat obscure relationship.

Besides distinct orders and ranks, Gaulish society may also have had various other social subdivisions, such as age groups, which boys entered when they reached puberty. Young males of the same age, especially stripling warriors, probably spent much of their time hanging out together, naturally preferring the company of the young to that of their elders. Here we envisage something akin to the 3rd-century *Gaesatae*, small bands of landless, young Gaulish warriors who lived outside the tribal structure, divorced from the everyday round of social and domestic activity. With no sure prospects but the potential for adventurism, a societal institution such as this may have provided a safety valve for restless, budding blades to seek their fame and fortune beyond their tribe for a limited time. It is plausible that such adventurous young warriors provided the initial recruits for Vercingetorix's cause.

CHRONOLOGY

What follows is a very brief and selective treatment of Caesar's *commentarii*, designed to give some idea of Caesar's movements (according to his own testimony) during his eight campaigning seasons in Gaul.

Commentarius	Year	Events
I	58 BC	Having raised from scratch two legions (*XI, XII*) in Italy, thus bringing his total to six legions, Caesar campaigned against the Helvetii, who Poseidonios described as 'rich in gold but a peaceful people' (*Geo.* 7.2.2). They were migrating en masse towards the fertile region of the Santones (Saintonge) in south-west Gaul and thus were regarded as a dangerous threat to the province of Gallia Transalpina. This movement west left their old homeland open to Germanic settlement. Unless Rome took Gaul, reasoned Caesar, the Germans would. Caesar finally defeated the Helvetii at Bibracte (Mont Beuvray) in a close-run battle.

Next he turned to the Germanic tribes under Ariovistus of the Suebi. Ironically, during Caesar's own consulship, the Senate had conferred the official but rather vague title of *socius et amicus populi Romani* to this tribe. Exploiting the rivalries between the Sequani and the Aedui, the latter a comparatively stable pro-Roman enclave on the fringe of Roman territory, the Germans crossed the upper Rhenus (Rhine) to seize the lands of these two north-eastern Gaulish tribes. Caesar understood that to succeed in Gaul he needed to eliminate this migratory element from the equation. Ariovistus, a man of marked ability, quickly outflanked Caesar and then sat squarely on his line of communications. The thunderstruck Caesar was compelled to regain his line of retreat, but finally managed to force a battle on the Germans. After a brutal contest, Caesar defeated them and drove the few survivors of the tribe across the Rhine.

Caesar had made blunders that in later campaigns he would not repeat. He left his legions in winter quarters among the Sequani far to the north of the formal boundary of Gallia Transalpina, and himself returned to Gallia Cisalpina. It would be his habit throughout the campaigns to spend the winter months there, carrying out his judicial and administrative activities as governor as well as keeping a close eye on the politics of Rome.

| II | 57 BC | By this stage it was clear Caesar had decided on total conquest. He raised a further two legions (*XIII* and *XIIII*), bringing his army to eight legions (at which strength it remained until 54 BC). Caesar turned his attention to the subjugation of the Belgae. Some of them were settled on the shores of the (Oceanus Germanicus North Sea), and significant groups had been crossing to Britannia for several generations, establishing kingdoms there. Having beaten a substantial Belgic army near Bibrax (either Beaurieux or Vieux Laon) in the territory of the Remi, Caesar quickly moved northwards against the more remote Belgic tribes, the Nervii and the Aduatuci. |

The fierce and warrior-like Nervii proclaimed they would rather accept death than Roman domination and criticized other tribes for having done so. The Nervii surprised Caesar at the Sabis river (Sambre) in an ambush, and almost annihilated his forces. He learned to be more cautious after this. Simultaneously, Publius Licinius Crassus, son of the triumvir Marcus, had campaigned against the Veneti and other maritime tribes that bordered upon the Atlantic between the mouth of the Seine and the Liger (Loire) estuary. The encirclement of Gaul was thus completed. However, Caesar recognized that he had more to do, as the legions were kept in the north, probably along the Loire, throughout that winter.

| III | 56 BC | Caesar's rumoured invasion of Britannia prompted the Veneti to rise up. Strabo wrote |

III   56 BC   Caesar's rumoured invasion of Britannia prompted the Veneti to rise up. Strabo wrote (*Geo.* 4.4.1) that the reason for the Venetic revolt was to hinder Caesar's voyage to Britannia, and protect their trade there. As befitting the strongest of the maritime tribes of Gaul, the Veneti were skilful seamen, had a powerful ocean-going fleet of oak-built, sailing ships and held the monopoly of the carrying trade with southern Britannia. Both Caesar's own *commentarius* and the archaeological record support this statement. British goods were exchanged for luxury imports, the most significant one being Italian wine shipped to the island in large ceramic amphorae (of the Dressel IA type). The reverse traffic would have included metals, in particular tin, together with grain, cattle, slaves, hides and hunting dogs (Strabo *Geo.* 4.5.2). The real reason for the revolt probably lay in the fact that the submissions extracted in the previous year by Publius Licinius were all but nominal.

Caesar's attempts to attack by land proved abortive, as many of the Venetic strongholds were built on isolated spits of land often only accessible by sea. However, one of his most able legates, Decimus Iunius Brutus Albinus (who would later play a key role in Caesar's assassination, alongside the more famous Marcus Brutus), overcame the Veneti at sea using a fleet constructed for the occasion. Caesar, with needless cruelty it seems, put the whole of the elder council to the sword and sold the tribe into slavery. Publius Licinius, meanwhile, had subdued some of the tribes of Aquitania. Towards the end of the campaigning season, Caesar himself led an attack on the Morini and the Menapii, tribes of the Belgae on the North Sea littoral who had not yet surrendered. They quickly withdrew into their forests, creating difficulties for Caesar. The onset of bad weather forced him to pull back.

IV   55 BC   Caesar started the season campaigning in Illyricum (in the Balkan region) against the Pirustae, who had been raiding Roman territory. He then defeated the Usipetes and the Tencteri, two Germanic tribes that had been crowded across the Rhine by the Suebi, the strongest nation on the eastern bank. Caesar marched against them, and was met by an offer of peace. Caesar alleged treachery on their part in the negotiations, but his own version in the fourth *commentarius* does not support this. During a brief armistice, Caesar's men marched upon the tribesmen and vanquished them. A few thousand survivors managed to escape across the river. In faraway Rome, Cato was so indignant at this act of unnecessary brutality that he proposed in the Senate to send Caesar in chains to the tribal survivors for punishment (*Caes.* 22.3). No notice was taken of his proposal.

Caesar then decided to intimidate the Germanic tribes further. More a publicity stunt than a punitive sortie, this trans-Rhine campaign was directed against the Sugambri. As much an engineering genius as a master soldier, in just ten days Caesar had built a trestle bridge across the Rhine near present day Coblenz. The first Roman invasion of Germania lasted a mere 18 days with much destruction inflicted and fear instilled. Despite the season being well advanced, Caesar conducted a raid against the Belgic tribes of south-eastern Britannia with two veteran legions (*VII, X*) and 500 horsemen. He risked everything by leading an under-strength and poorly supplied force to an unknown land across a boisterous sea. Caesar landed at a point 7 Roman miles (10.36km) west of modern Dover, variously identified as present day Lympne in Romney Marsh, or between Walmer Castle and Deal.

It could be said that one of his greatest traits as a general – *celeritas*, or quickness of action – became a burden. Yet Caesar was an adventurer and showman who could not resist the lure of the unknown. Some battles were fought, some settlements burnt and some hostages taken. Back home the publicity was excellent as Britannia was represented as 'beyond the Ocean', which had certainly limited the ambitions of Alexander the Great. Even Cicero was caught up in the hype, planning to write an epic poem on the 'glorious conquest', based on front-line reports from his brother Quintus (*Att.* 4.16.7, 18.5).

| V | 54 BC | With a much better prepared plan of campaign, Caesar returned to Britannia with five legions (over half his total army) and 2,000 horsemen. He landed unopposed somewhere between what is now Sandown and Sandwich, reached the Tamesis (Thames) and defeated Cassivellaunus of the Catuvellauni, a Gallo-Belgic tribe. At the time he was one of the most powerful people of Britannia; the aggressive behaviour of the Catuvellauni towards other tribes had already become notorious. |

However, on his return to Gaul in the autumn Caesar was faced with a major revolt of the Belgae and the Treveri precipitated by the charismatic war leader, Ambiorix of the Eburones, a small but hardy tribe in the Arduenna Silva (Ardennes). In the flurry of events that ensued, *legio XIIII* (one of the newest formations) and five cohorts of raw recruits (perhaps the core of a new legion), under the joint command of the two legates Lucius Aurunculeius Cotta and Quintus Titurius Sabinus, were surrounded and all but annihilated. Was this a case of poor leadership? The massacre of Roman troops was a huge blow to Caesar's prestige, and it is with a hint of outrage that Caesar portrays Sabinus as an inept coward. Whatever the truth, it demonstrated to the Gauls for the first time that Caesar was not invincible. As a result, the Nervii were emboldened to mount a determined, but ultimately unsuccessful, formal siege of the winter camp held by Quintus Tullius Cicero, the orator's brother.

With hindsight, it is easy to argue that Caesar, who was relying on the supposed subjection of the Gauls, had quartered his legions unwisely far apart. With his usual luck and brilliance, however, he managed to save the situation from disaster. Yet the troops posted in their winter camps among the Belgae must have been feeling distinctly uneasy, and the recent events were a firm reminder to all and sundry that Gaul was by no means conquered. Further armed rebellions, even more serious, were to follow.

| VI | 53 BC | Following the disastrous winter, the campaigning season's efforts concentrated on re-establishing Roman control in north-eastern Gaul. Vicious punitive strikes against the recalcitrant Nervii forced them to surrender. Operations followed against the northerly Menapii, which forced them to submit for the first time, and the Treveri. Caesar built a second bridge close to the first location, and led a punitive expedition over the Rhine to punish the Germanic tribes for having aided the Gauls. But supply problems and an unwillingness to face the Suebi limited the scope of Caesar's operations. His forays into Germanic territory were much like the medieval *chevauchée* – a raid to intimidate opponents, demonstrate the power of your army and convince those sitting on the fence to come down and support your side. The elusive Ambiorix of the Eburones managed to slip away with a small band of horsemen, and was never caught. |

One aspect of this year's campaigning was Caesar's need to bring the Senones and Carnutes to heel. Both tribes occupied land south of the Seine and hitherto had been left largely unmolested. This action was likely mounted because these tribes were providing safe havens for dissidents. Moreover, Caesar tells us that the druids met annually in the territory of the Carnutes, the 'centre' of all Gaul; they were seen as the one power that could unite the Gauls. Caesar's relentless war of attrition continued. In the long term Roman discipline and Caesar's ability to regroup and bring up reserves could not fail against a foe distracted by jarring factions and weakened by the devastation of their crops and herds.

By the end of the year Caesar had increased his army to ten legions with the formation of two units (*XIIII* and *XV* – the former replacing the 'lost' *XIIII*) and the borrowing of another from Pompey (*legio I*, which had been part of his consular army of 55 BC). As the year drew to a close, some 2,000 Sugambrian horsemen crossed the Rhine and raided Gaul. They also attacked Caesar's central supply base at Aduatuca (somewhere near modern day Tongeren, Belgium) where his sick and wounded were recuperating, under the protection of the green and raw *legio XIIII*. Only the heroism of individuals, especially centurions, saved the day.

VII	52 BC	Over the winter months Caesar flung the doors open to non-citizens, enrolling recruits in Gallia Transalpina; this was the genesis of the famed *legio V Alaudae*, with another legion, numbered *VI*, being brought into service a little later in the year. In theory, Roman citizens alone were eligible for legionary service. Citizens or not, these *tiro* legionaries were going to be needed. From 58 BC onwards Caesar conquered more Gaulish territory each year, but the year 52 BC very nearly marked Caesar's military nadir. He found himself confronting an armed rebellion by almost all the Gaulish tribes under the command of their elected war leader, Vercingetorix. The two armies were to clash at Avaricum and Gergovia, then again at Alesia. The latter would become a graveyard for one of them.
VIII	51 BC	The opening words of the eighth *commentarius*, 'The whole of Gaul was now conquered', were true to a point. Although Gaul was now completely under Roman control, there were still pockets of discontent that Caesar and his legates had to deal with. In the north, among the Belgae, the Bellovaci made a nuisance of themselves by threatening the clients of Rome's traditional allies the Remi. Come springtime, Caesar marched to Belgica to suppress the Bellovaci. His show of strength dealt a final blow to latent Belgic resistance. Aulus Hirtius, who now takes up the story, mentions a concerted plan, but these troubles appeared to be nothing other than the backwash of Alesia.

The last remaining serious resistance was in the south-west where Drappes, a Senonian with influence among other tribes, and Lucterius, a local Cadurcan, took over the well-fortified *oppidum* of Uxellodunum (Puy d'Issolu) overlooking the Duranius (Dordogne). The stronghold fell after Caesar cut off its water supply. To put a stop to further revolts, and doubtless to remind the natives of the benefits of Roman overlordship, Caesar ordered the hands of all those who had borne arms against him to be cut off. This atrocity thus brought the conquest of Gaul to its bitter end. The rest of the campaign season was spent mopping up, sometimes with great ruthlessness, the many pockets of resistance that still remained. By the end of his last year in Gaul Caesar was able to return to Gallia Cisalpina content in the knowledge that his conquests and achievements would survive.

OPPOSING COMMANDERS

Some of the aspects that make the composition of a detailed military biography of Vercingetorix difficult include the fact that he lived in a pre-literate society, and that his military career was very brief and somewhat unsuccessful. For Caesar, by contrast, we do at least have his well-known memoirs.

Caesar's campaigns in Gaul were moves in a power game, one in which his ambition was on a collision course both with the Senate and his great rival Pompey. Although his conquests there were technically illegal (he had no such mandate from the Senate), as an audacious and astute politician he was aware of the importance – the necessity – of the semblance of legality, and needed to maintain favourable public opinion back home. It is to this need for self-justification (and indeed publicity) that we owe the publication of his *commentarii*.

VERCINGETORIX

It is difficult to know what to make of Vercingetorix from this distance, for his career was both too short and too shadowy for anything but a summary account. This is especially so because he is primarily known to us through Caesar's *commentarii*. The singular, glittering thread of Vercingetorix's history is therein laid out in various passages, playing second fiddle to the great author.

Vercingetorix's father Celtillus, we are told, had tried to make himself king, but had been killed by his compatriots in factional fighting. Setting oneself up as a king was an offence punishable by death among the more socially advanced tribes of Gaul, and by Caesar's day hereditary kinship had been abandoned in favour of elected magistrates. Caesar (*BG* 7.4.5) hints that Vercingetorix held monarchical ambitions. He was therefore something of a social pariah who had nothing to gain from conforming; leading an armed rebellion against Rome, however, had much to offer this ambitious young dissident.

Vercingetorix had independently recruited to his cause bands of young warriors from diverse tribes. In Caesar's own choice phrase they are dismissed as 'down-and-outs and desperadoes' (*BG* 7.4.3), a gang of outlaws. Once many of the tribes had pledged support for him, Vercingetorix quickly got to work and prepared for a showdown with Rome. He was a great speaker, and easily won the approval of Gaulish warriors, which they customarily demonstrated by clashing their weapons. He was also a shrewd campaigner,

Spectacular bronze sculpture of an idealized Vercingetorix, Place de Jaude, Clermont-Ferrand, by Fédéric Auguste Bartholdi (1834–1904) – who sculpted the Statue of Liberty. The patrician Caesar was one of those rare types that not only made the history but reported it too. To him, of course, the Arvernian war leader was little more than a troublesome rebel. Since the mid-19th century, Vercingetorix has been represented as a flawless patriot, as an accomplished leader, and as a symbol of Gallic resistance to the threat of external encroachment, real or imagined. Like most good legends, the one that surrounds him is not totally unfounded, but the bare facts of his life are rather less colourful than the language of folklore. Nonetheless, he did make one unwitting contribution to modern France: he gave (along with Jeanne d'Arc) the country a sense of national identity. (Fabien 1309)

not prone to impetuosity like so many Gaulish chieftains, insulated as they were within their local little worlds of feuds and forays. He was to prove himself more than a match for Caesar in strategy. During his defence of Gergovia (near Clermont-Ferrand) it is interesting to read that each morning at first light Vercingetorix assembled his war chiefs in council and allotted them their daily tasks, much like a modern military commander (*BG* 7.36.3).

Yet he was also cruel, as witnessed by the putting out of eyes, the amputation of limbs and the burnings at the stake that he ordered – according to Caesar's account (*BG* 7.4.9). Florus' version is slightly different. He says that Vercingetorix was a 'chief formidable alike for his stature, his skill in arms, and his courage, endowed too, with a name which seemed to be intended to inspire terror' (*Epit.* 1.45.21) – the generally accepted view is that Vercingetorix literally means either 'great warrior king' or 'king of great warriors'. Pure terror, or was it a matter of plain trust? Amongst the Gauls diversity was more obvious than uniformity, tribal autonomy more obvious than national interdependence. The concept of one people, one law, one tongue did not apply in Gaul.

Soon after the Roman reverse at Gergovia and the defection of the Aedui, a great council was convened at Bibracte (Mont Beuvray), the principal *oppidum* of that tribe. It was here that a popular vote unanimously confirmed Vercingetorix as the supreme commander of the combined rebel forces (*BG* 7.63.6). For Gaulish arms this represented a staggering achievement, for Caesar a massive blow to his personal prestige. The summer thus approached and the rebellion still held. Its strongest bolt was Vercingetorix's undisputed military leadership.

CAESAR

Caesar was monotonous and thorough, and he was dogged. He possessed all the qualities of a warlord, including the absolute moral indifference that is necessary to such a part. As a conqueror he certainly cuts a controversial figure. Whatever reservations may be held about this side of his character, he certainly possessed that rare combination of being an inspiring leader, a good general and an expert fighting man. His peculiarly daring personality instantly won the confidence of his men. At Alesia Caesar would demonstrate the qualities that made men follow him under adverse conditions. He was fit, both mentally and physically, energetic and confident, capable of making rapid decisions but also willing to listen to his senior centurions. His soldiers seldom saw him ruffled and he was always ready for a simple joke. His shrewd use of ground, sound tactics and willingness to take the supreme gamble would bring him victory.

With the conquest of Gaul Caesar's ambition would come to fruition. Yet it is important to remember that when Caesar left for Gaul, his practical military experience had been minimal. He certainly had very little experience at the head of legions, a deficiency he partly made up by taking Titus Atius Labienus as a *legatus pro praetore*, a seasoned soldier usually described as Caesar's second-in-command and right-hand man. As far as we know, Caesar had not been involved in any major pitched battle before, although he had seen plenty of smaller actions. These had included a fascinating, private encounter with pirates as a young man (75 BC), a short participation as a junior officer in Asia, and Cilicia (Second Mithridatic War, 83–81 BC), where he was to win the *corona civica* for saving the life of a fellow soldier at the storming of Mytilene (81 BC). It is possible he saw some action as a military tribune sometime during the Third Servile War (73–71 BC), a detestable war of ambushes and inglorious surprises. Also, a few years before his Gallic command, he had tasted all the uncertainties of guerrilla warfare first hand as *propraetor* in Iberia (61–60 BC). The lessons he drew and later applied were that unity was strength, safety lay in numbers and military professionalism was power – simple to state, difficult to accomplish.

It was there in Hispania Ulterior, Suetonius relates, that Caesar visited a shrine in Gades (Cadiz) and gazed upon a statue of Alexander. He sighed that, at his age, 'Alexander had already conquered the whole world' (*DI* 7). Indeed, in 30 years the dashing Macedonian world conqueror had filled three men's full lifetimes. On the other hand, the 40-year-old Caesar was not yet a

Jules César, a neoclassical marble statue (Paris, Jardin des Tuileries, inv. 2099) by the sculptor Ambrogio Parisi (1676–1719). This statue of Caesar was commissioned in 1694 for le parc de Versailles; its bearing (and baton) is somewhat reminiscent of the Sun King, Louis XIV. Ruler of France and warlord for more than seven decades, Louis led his armies in his youth but, unlike Caesar, who remains the ideal of a Roman general, he never fought a major battle. However, both men bought their glory with needless destruction and effusion of innocent blood.
(© Esther Carré)

master of the military craft. He had seen 'the tip of the wolf's ear' but not its jaws.

Most great generals of ancient times gained their laurels while still young. The father of Alexander, Philip of Macedon, ascended the throne at the age of 22, and soon distinguished himself in his wars with the neighbouring states. At the age of 45 he had conquered all Greece. He died at 47. Alexander himself had defeated the celebrated Theban Sacred Band at the battle of Chaironeia, and gained a military reputation at the age of 18. He ascended the throne of his father Philip before 20, and immediately entered on that career of world conquest that immortalized his name. At 25 he had reached the zenith of his military fame, having already conquered the known world. He died before the age of 33. Caesar, on the other hand, was 52 when he won the field of Pharsalus. At the opening of the civil war his opponent Pompey appeared at the head of the army at the advanced age of 59. Having lost the vigour and fire of youth, Pompey would achieve little of importance, and lose his life in the process.

In battle a Roman commander needed to be able to exercise control over his army at all times. He needed to be close enough to read the battle, but not too close so as to get sucked into the initial fight. Caesar typically rode close behind the front line of his army. From this sensible position he encouraged his men, witnessed their behaviour and rewarded or punished them accordingly. He also had a close view of the combat zone and could appreciate the situation as the thousands battled, judging the fight by the morale exhibited and the communication of friend and foe alike. Using this information he could feed in reinforcements from his second or third lines to exploit a success or relieve part of the fighting line that was under pressure. Put simply, Caesar had tactical *coup d'oeil*, that is to say, the ability to perceive the decisive point, even the need to intervene personally in the fight when his army was on the verge of defeat or when the moment had arrived to move in for the kill. Caesar's appreciation that personal intervention in battle was not considered incompatible with the demands of leadership can be seen in his praise of the doomed Lucius Aurunculeius Cotta for fulfilling the duties of a commander and fighting in the ranks as a common soldier during his annihilation at the hands of the Belgae and the Treveri.

Just as the function of a Roman soldier was to fight battles, the function of a Roman commander was to win them. He therefore needed to judge where and when the crisis of battle would occur and move to that part of the fighting line. There is no doubt that in this function Caesar took up prudent positions to ensure he reacted positively and instinctively. Yet often we find him next to his soldiers, exposing life and limb to mortal danger.

When the day's outcome was in doubt, Caesar would send away his horse as a grand gesture, clearly demonstrating that he, like his men, could not escape from the enemy's blows and that he was ready to die alongside them (*BG* 1.25.1). Caesar understood his soldiers, much like his uncle Caius Marius. He shared with them the glories and the rewards, but also the toils, miseries and, above all, the dangers of soldiering. He was indifferent to personal comforts or luxuries. Since boyhood he had been an expert horseman, and had trained himself to ride at full gallop with both hands clasped behind his back. During the campaigns in Gaul he even got into the habit of dictating dispatches while on horseback.

If Caesar was a risk taker, he was one who carefully hedged his bets. When stepping into a fight, the decision was taken either by necessity or by the certainty that his appearance would stiffen the resolve of his men. In the unrelenting head-to-head fighting on the banks of the Sabis against the Nervii in 57 BC, Caesar's army was caught totally unprepared while making camp; it would be his splendid example of bravery that would help save the day. At Alesia, in contrast, Caesar led the final attack as the enemy were on the verge of overrunning his siege lines. When his soldiers realized that Caesar himself was coming, they fought with greater vigour and won the day.

There were of course considerable risks when demonstrating such direct leadership on the battlefield. Caesar clearly understood that command must be singular, and that only when momentum was required to assure victory (or in a desperate and doomed last stand) should the commander enter the forefront of the fighting.

Whatever sort of conqueror Caesar was, there is no question that he was superbly equipped for the role. His strategic and tactical flair, his personal leadership, his speed and use of surprise – as well as copious amounts of good luck – were on conspicuous display.

OPPOSING ARMIES

Caesar's greatest asset of all was arguably the Roman army, which had been reformed by his uncle Marius in 107 BC. Whilst according Caesar his due glory, it is important to emphasize the fact that he did not introduce any significant innovations in the pragmatic, professional army of his day. By contrast, what was ornamental in warfare was in the hands of the Gauls. Indeed, the tumultuous, trousered warriors streaming in one barbaric surge towards the Roman siege lines at Alesia must have been ornamental as lime, enamel, glass, silver and gold could make them. For the Romans the notion of 'adornment' suggested the superficial, the superfluous, even the frivolous. The rationale of the Gauls, however, was rather different. For them, the decorated appearance was more often thought to reveal rather than conceal. With no concept of a professional army in the Gaulish world, almost any free man could find himself involved in military action. Besides, as Strabo noted, 'the whole race is war-mad, and both high-spirited and quick for battle' (*Geo.* 4.4.2).

VERCINGETORIX'S ARMY

The Gauls had a fearsome reputation for aggressiveness, even among the militaristic Romans. There can be no doubt that warfare played a central role in Gaulish society, a society that was tribal, hierarchical and familiar. For the nobles and their warriors, raiding offered the opportunity of wealth, prestige and reputation to further political aspirations at home. As was the case in Germania, armed retinues could only be maintained by actual fighting and they seem to have been at least semi-permanent. Added to their clients, they formed a strong nucleus for the tribal army. Polybios, writing much earlier about the Gauls, notes that nobles 'treated comradeship as of great importance, those among them being the most feared and most powerful who were thought to have the largest number of attendants and associates' (2.17.12). These elite warriors were, however, far outnumbered by the mass of ordinary warriors, whose ranks were composed of all free tribesmen able to equip themselves. Here we must remember that the majority of Vercingetorix's people, even though bound to a local chieftain by dues of clan service, were farmers who planted crops and raised cattle. There would have been a few raw youths and greying men feeling their years too.

This tribesman appears to have gone to war in a band based on clan, familial or settlement groupings, which made his fellow men into witnesses

Mouth of a Celtic war trumpet known as the *carnyx*, found in November 2004 in a Gaulish sanctuary at Tintignac (*département* of Corrèze), and dated to the 1st century BC. Wrought in sheet bronze, it is in the form of a serpent's head. Its eyes would have been inserts made of brightly coloured enamel. Four other *carnyxes* were in the deposit, all of which had mouths in the manner of the more familiar stylized boar. The Tintignac *carnyxes* ended their lives as a sacrifice, a ritual offering to some unknown god, not long after Caesar's conquest. (Claude Valette)

of his behaviour. It is likely too that the boldest (or more foolhardy) and best equipped naturally gravitated to the front rank of a war band. Equipment in general was fairly scanty, the combination of shield with an iron boss, long slashing sword and short thrusting spear(s) forming the war gear of most warriors. Body armour seems to have been very rare, and a warrior probably went into the fray dressed only in a pair of loose woollen trousers.

The appearance of the individual, his size, expressions and demoniacal war cries, added to the din of clashing weapons and the harsh braying of the *carnyx* (war trumpet), were clearly intended to intimidate the enemy before actually reaching them. Diodorus writes, 'their trumpets are of a peculiar kind, they blow into them and produce a harsh sound that suits the tumult of war' (DS 5.30.3). Similarly at Alesia, 'from all directions shouting and howling [*clamore et ululate*] went up from the Gauls' (*BG* 7.80.4). Such brouhaha was sufficiently startling and cacophonous to set the enemy on edge.

If any were persuaded that he was going to lose before an actual mêlée began, then a Gaulish charge, oftentimes launched without warning, would drive all before it. Gaulish war bands were not subtle. Tactics – if tactics we may call them – were unsophisticated, and relied on a wild, headlong rush by a churning mass of yelling warriors in a rough phalangial order headed by their war leaders, followed up by deadly close-up work with ashen spear and long sword. As was common in tribal armies, the unmilitary (but exceedingly warlike) warriors were poorly disciplined and lacked training above the level of the individual; drill and discipline of the Roman kind were regarded as foreign trickery unworthy of Gaulish warriors. And so, after a violent and savage onslaught launched amid a colossal din, the individual warrior battered his way into the enemy's ranks, smashing with his shield, stabbing with his spear or slashing with his sword. The muscular agility of Gaulish warriors was a thing to behold, and those on the opposing side could only stand like pebbles on a beach, waiting for the smothering surge. Yet while such aggression was paramount, intending to startle and scatter the enemy, it was apparent that autarkic heroism by itself was insufficient against an army as efficient as Caesar's.

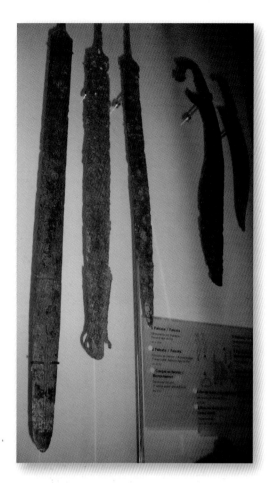

Three Gaulish long slashing swords (Paris, Musée d'armée, inv. B 37276, B 30a, B 30b) recovered from Cernon-sur-Coole (*département* of Marne), and dated to the end of La Tène period (La Tène D, 150–30 BC). (© Esther Carré)

One thing is certain about Vercingetorix's army: it was a rambunctious host, containing as its flower some of the best manpower any Gaulish warrior ever saw. The warriors were raw-boned, sinewy men used to handling weapons and to the outdoor life, men who could get along very well on poor rations and skimpy equipment. They comprised bands of free tribesmen who were fit, agile and extremely belligerent with a positive taste for fighting. Like all tribal warriors, they were shrewd, quick-witted, wary, cunning and ready for all emergencies. While there was no attempt at discipline, their courage was tempestuous, excitable, self-conscious.

Still, it was horsemen that provided the highest quality warriors in any Gaulish army. They were drawn chiefly from the nobles – the *equites* mentioned by Caesar – and their retinues and clients. Given that they were recruited from the wealthier and more prestigious warriors, equipment was of good quality and consisted of a shield, one or two javelins, a short spear, the ubiquitous long slashing sword, and often helmet and mail armour. Added to this was the four-horned saddle, later adopted by the Romans, a key technical innovation that provided a thoroughly secure seat. The morale of these horse bands was usually very high. For instance, even when outclassed by the Parthian *cataphractarii* (completely armoured horsemen) at Carrhae in 53 BC, the Gaulish horse under Publius Crassus (son of Marcus) displayed their prowess in horsemanship and fought fiercely (*Cras.* 25.3–10). Tactics were normally straightforward: a shower of javelins was thrown, followed up by a charge using spears and swords. Discipline was normally poor, so that they were difficult to rally from pursuit or rout.

Polybios describes (2.33.3, cf. 30.8) how some Gaulish slashing swords were made of poor metal; sometimes they bent on impact, thereby requiring the owner to retire and stamp the blade back into shape with his foot before re-entering the fray. This view is contradicted by the archaeological record, which suggests Gaulish words were very well made with a good edge and great flexibility. Other authors took up Polybios' comments and criticisms (for example, Plutarch *Camillus* 41.4, Polyainos 8.7.2). The one shining exception was Philon of Byzantium (*fl. c.*200 BC) who, in an illuminating passage written around the time of Polybios' birth, describes how the Gauls test the excellence of their swords:

> They grasp the hilt in the right hand and the end of the blade in the left: then, laying it horizontally on their heads, they pull down at each end until [the ends] touch their shoulders. Next, they let go sharply, removing both hands. When released, it straightens itself out again and so resumes its original shape, without retaining a suspicion of a bend. Though they repeat this frequently, the swords remain straight. (*Belo.* 4.71)

Swords exhibited various general and local fashions during the La Tène period. Blades were short from the 5th to the 3rd century BC. Improvements in iron technology and changes in fighting style resulted in the two-edged sword designed for slashing, often of enormous length and round-ended, from the 2nd to the 1st century BC. Surviving examples of this period have an overall length range of about 850 to 900mm, with some having a blade length of 900mm without the handle. Few of these blades descend to the poor quality described by Polybios.

Graeco-Roman commentators found the length of the Gaulish sword remarkable, as exemplified by Diodorus Sicolus' comments: 'Instead of the short sword [the *gladius*] they carry long swords held by a chain of iron or bronze and hanging along their right flank' (DS 5.30.3). They found Gaulish swordplay singular too. Being blunt ended, the Gaulish sword could be used only for slashing and not for thrusting, 'which is the peculiar and only stroke of the Gauls' (DS 2.33.5). Thus, the Gauls 'raised their arms aloft and smote, throwing the whole weight of their bodies into the blows as if they intended to cut the bodies of their opponents into pieces' (DH 14.10.1).

In the hands of a tall Gaulish warrior with a long reach, the weapon could be a deadly blade, especially against Roman legionaries with their shorter *gladii*. The Gaulish slashing sword, unlike the Roman *gladius*, did not derive its killing power from collective use, but rather from the individual skill and strength of the man who wielded the weapon. Little wonder, therefore, that the sword was considered the weapon of the high status warrior, and that to carry one was to display a symbol of rank and prestige. Perhaps surprisingly it was worn on the right, suspended from a bronze or iron chain around the waist. The chain passed through a suspension loop on the back of the

Reconstructed Gaulish long slashing sword (MuséoParc Alésia). Such an extraordinary long sword, and blunt ended to boot, required a warrior to have a fair amount of elbow room on the field of battle in order to operate proficiently. Nonetheless, those who could expertly swing one of these made fearsome opponents for other men. Even the most grizzled, battle-hardened legionary veteran would likely have felt fear if a sword-swinging Gaul got close enough to slash him. (© Esther Carré)

Gaulish waist-belt of iron chain (Niort, Musée ethnographique et archéologique du Donjon) found at Faye-l'Abbesse (*département* of Deux-Sèvres), and dated to the beginning of La Tène period (La Tène A, 460–400 BC). Belts were often worn, particularly the waist-belt of the warrior, which was generally a chain of bronze or iron. According to Strabo (quoting Ephoros), the Gauls would 'endeavour not to grow fat or potbellied' (*Geo.* 4.4.6), adding that a fine was imposed upon those who became too obese to do up their belts. Perhaps surprisingly, swords were worn on the right-hand side, with the waist-belt passing through a suspension loop on the back of the scabbard. It is in fact fairly easy to draw even a long blade from this position. Roman legionaries, likewise, wore their swords on the right. (© Esther Carré)

scabbard and kept the weapon upright, helping to prevent the sword from becoming entangled with the warrior's legs as he walked or ran. In fact, it is fairly easy to draw even a long blade from this position. A Gaulish warrior, when swinging his long slashing sword, was unquestionably happiest when moving forward on the attack. The target areas for such a fearsome weapon were the head, shoulders (if visible), the right arm and the left leg. It was certainly not contrived for finesse, but was designed to either hack an opponent to pieces or to beat him to a bloody pulp.

CAESAR'S ARMY

Caesar's own elegantly and lucidly written account of his campaigns gives us an invaluable picture of the Roman army in this period. However, he does generally assume that his reader is well acquainted with all the necessary detailed information about the army's command-structure, equipment and tactics. To labour such details would have been trivial and pointless. To a modern readership, therefore, the technical details he provides may often be disappointingly sketchy, yet his depiction of the men under his command is one of the most prominent and distinctive features of his *commentarii*. Nothing in ancient literature corresponds to the prominence of these soldiers or their moral and military significance in the battle narratives.

The forces available to Caesar when he arrived in Gallia Cisalpina consisted of three legions, numbered in orderly sequence from *VII* to *VIIII*, with a further legion (*X*) in Gallia Transalpina. These legions were supported by a colourful range (of unspecified number) of auxiliaries, including Iberian horsemen, Numidian javelineers and perhaps some of their famed horsemen too, Cretan archers and Balearic slingers, along with a number of locally raised Gaulish troops, horsemen in the main and at one time numbering at least 5,000 (*BG* 4.12.1). In the campaign of 52 BC Caesar had some Germanic horsemen. According to the Germanic custom, these horsemen were accompanied by a similar number of nimble foot warriors who were trained

Legionaries on the Altar of Domitius Ahenobarbus (Paris, musée du Louvre, inv. Ma 975) equipped with the typical arms and armour of the late Republic. Like today's infantryman, Caesar's legionary was a most workmanlike figure, his appearance almost 'base and beggarly' by later Principate standards. Much of the success of the Roman army on the battlefield lay in the soldier's knowledge of close formation fighting. Legionaries were trained to fight as a team, to trust each other and to remain steady under pressure. It was this difference that gave the legion its decisive tactical edge. (© Esther Carré)

to fight among their ranks (*BG* 1.48, 7.65.4). Obviously these men had to be fit, fast moving and versatile. The importance of these Germanic allies should not be underestimated. At Alesia, as we shall witness in due course, their actions would be crucial, if not decisive.

We know nothing about the previous history of Caesar's legions, except that they were already in his provinces when he took up his command. Under the legislation appointing him to the command, the *lex Vatinia* of 59 BC, he was allowed a *quaestor* to handle the financial affairs of his army, and ten *legati* (legates) whom he could appoint directly, without reference to the Senate (*Vat.* 35–6). During the eight years Caesar was campaigning in Gaul, he would increase his army from four to twelve legions, all of which were under his direct command. Most of the new recruits were probably volunteers. All the new formations were raised over the wintertime in Caesar's own provinces, though some Italians presumably travelled north on their own account, with a view to enlistment. The new legions were raised by virtue, it would seem, of a proconsul's right to call out local forces in defence of his province.

At first Caesar paid and equipped the new legions at his own expense from the profits of war. At the Luca conference in April 56 BC he was able to get recognition for legions *XI–XIIII*, which were henceforth paid by state funds, but later formations remained dependent for pay on Caesar himself. He enlisted men both south and north of the river Po. Though there were Roman citizens in Gallia Cisalpina, many of those living north of the river were not, having the lesser status of 'Latins'. Caesar ignored the distinction, and was happy to admit all to his ranks. Hence the formation of a militia from the native population of Gallia Transalpina, 22 cohorts in all, which formed the basis of *legio V Alaudae* that we later find among his forces. Existing legions were supplemented each year by drafts from Gallia Cisalpina, so that by the time Caesar crossed the Rubicon, his army must have possessed a unique coherence and loyalty, important factors in his eventual victory.

Although Caesar himself did little to reform the army, he did raise the soldiers under his command to a peak of efficiency. He trained his men hard,

Drawing of Minucius Lorarius, as depicted on his grave stele (Padua, Museo Civico di Padova), discovered in Via Orus, Padua. The stele possibly dates to either 43 BC or 42 BC. The fact that Lorarius is holding a *vitis* (vine stick) tells us that he was a centurion. Other than his antiquated greaves, and perhaps a helmet adorned with a transverse crest, *crista traversa*, a centurion of this period was equipped pretty much like his men. He did, however, carry his *gladius* (sword) on his left rather than his right hip, perhaps to keep it clear of the *vitis* (see detail, below). The stele's mutilated inscription gives Lorarius' unit as *legio Martia* (its exact numeral is unknown – *III*, *XIII* or *XXIII*?). 'Martia' meant 'sacred to Mars' and, according to Appian, the legion 'took its cognomen from its reputation for valour' (*Bellum civilia* 4.115). Lorarius may have been killed fighting against Marcus Antonius at Forum Gallorum (14 April 43 BC), or drowned in the Adriatic (summer 42 BC) when the legion, en route to Philippi to fight the tyrannicides, was tragically lost at sea. (Drawn by Steven D. P. Richardson)

LEFT
Bronze Montefortino helmet (Bad Deutsch-Altenburg, Archaeological Museum Carnuntum), dated to the 1st century BC. Its cheek pieces are missing but their hinges are obvious. (Matthias Kabel)

RIGHT
Full-scale reconstruction of a bronze Montefortino helmet (MuséoParc Alésia), complete with cheek pieces and horsetail plume. Based on a Celtic design, this helmet pattern was basically a hemispherical bowl beaten to shape, with a narrow peaked neck guard, large cheek pieces and an integral crest knob, which was filled with lead to secure a crest pin. The Montefortino was the most successful helmet type ever designed, winning almost total acceptance in the Roman army, where it was used virtually unchanged for nearly four centuries. The curved shape of the helmet helped to deflect sword blows and arrows. Other common features include a rope-type design around the rim, and pinecone-type patterning on the crest knob. (© Esther Carré)

but also flattered them, fostering their pride in themselves and their unit. He created an especially close bond with the crack *legio X Equestris*, habitually placing them on the right of his battleline, the position of most honour. Moreover, he led them in person, all of which turned them into a proto-praetorian guard. Such flattery and favours not only ensured its staunch loyalty to him, but also made it one of the fiercest fighting formations of his army. Being Caesar's most trusted force had a negative side, though; it encouraged their narcissism, stimulated their sense of elite status and fostered their feeling of self-importance and indispensability. When this veteran legion, physically and psychologically worn out by long service in the Gallic and civil wars, threatened to mutiny, Caesar restored order with a single, barked word, addressing them as *quirites*, civilians not soldiers. Normally commanders began addresses to their men with *milites*, soldiers. Caesar habitually began with the more flattering term *commilitones*, comrades, a term imbued with a feeling of brotherly loyalty and a sense of responsibility for the fate of his men. This inborn feeling of fraternity did not undermine Caesar's authority as leader; on the contrary, it served to enhance it. Yet now he was addressing his battle-hardened veterans as citizens, mere men off the street with no military worth. He was implying, of course, that he now considered them discharged from his service.

Possibly raised by Caesar personally when he was governor of Hispania Ulterior (61–60 BC), *legio X* was with him throughout the Gallic campaigns (58–49 BC), and would be again in Iberia (49 BC). It would also fight at Pharsalus (48 BC) and again at Thapsus (46 BC). The survivors were discharged en masse after 16 years' service (46–45 BC), but were fighting again at Munda (45 BC). The legion's emblem was the bull, perhaps reflecting its Caesarian origin; the bull was the zodiacal sign associated with Venus, legendary ancestress of the Iulii. It gained the cognomen *Equestris* after Caesar ordered part of the legion to mount up on the horses of his Gaulish cavalry and to accompany him to the parley with Ariovistus (58 BC). This prompted one wit among the soldiers to discern a further honour for this, already Caesar's favourite legion. For some time he had been treating the unit as his personal bodyguard, and now he was making all its members *equites* – the aristocratic cavalry traditionally provided by the equestrian order

(*BG* 1.48.2–10). Of course, the *equites* had long since abandoned any military function and had turned into the social rank just below the senators. The actual cavalry (also *equites*) of Caesar's day consisted of auxiliaries, that is, non-Romans of inferior status to citizen legionaries. So by transferring the men of *legio X*, joked the soldier, they were not being *de*moted but *pro*moted.

Although there was still no permanent legionary commander (a situation that would remain until the establishment of the Principate under Augustus), there were still, as in the days of Marius, six military tribunes, *tribuni militum*, in each legion. Likewise, tribunes were still elected by the citizens in the *comitia centuriata* (assembly of centuries), and the young Caesar had been elected tribune in this fashion. However, additional tribunes could be chosen by a commander himself. Here demands of *amicitia* ('friendship') were met by taking on to his staff family, friends and the sons of political associates, who were thereby able to acquire some military experience that would stand them in good stead for future excursions into politics. Cicero's friend Caius Trebatius was offered a tribunate by Caesar (*Fam.* 7.5.3, 8.1), and for young, inexperienced blue bloods such an appointment was the swiftest way of kick starting a political career in the *cursus honorum* (the sequential order of public offices).

It is important to note that there is no instance of a military tribune commanding a legion in action during Caesar's campaigns in Gaul. As they were invariably short-term politicos, who had an eye cast in the direction of Rome, tribunes could be something of an embarrassment at times. In 58 BC, when Caesar was preparing to march against the Suebic king Ariovistus, these young blades became so terrified that they tried to excuse themselves from duty and some even wept openly. Therefore, Caesar was probably uneasy with the traditional leadership of legions by military tribunes.

In their place Caesar started to appoint a senior officer, usually a legate (*legatus*, pl. *legati*), both for the command of individual legions and as a commander of an expeditionary force detached from the main army. Hence Caesar placed his *quaestor* and five *legati* in command of his six legions for the fight against Ariovistus, 'to act as witness of each man's valour' (*BG* 1.52.1). The *quaestor* was an elected magistrate, a senator at an early stage of his *cursus honorum* who was supposed to administer the finances of a province and act as a governor's deputy. Similarly, in the early winter of 54 BC when his army was distributed over Gaul because of the difficulty of the food supply, the various areas were entrusted to picked legates.

As previously noted, the *lex Vatinia* granted Caesar the right to appoint *legati* without a *senatus consultum*. Counting his second-in-command and his *quaestor*, senatorial appointments, Caesar had five *legati* in the years 58 BC to 55 BC, the number rising to ten in 54 BC, and to twelve in 52 BC. That they had *imperium pro praetore*, the powers of a propraetor, is not mentioned by Caesar, and perhaps only his second-in-command alone was so distinguished. Unlike most if not all military tribunes, these legates were not elected but chosen by Caesar from amongst his *amicitia*. Routinely of senatorial rank, some of these men might be former proconsular governors or army commanders, providing the leadership, experience and stability that

Buggenum type helmet (Trieste, Museo di Storia ed Arte di Trieste, inv. 3648), dated to the time of the triumvirate wars. With its larger, flatter neck guard and the addition of a brow-ridge to deflect downward blows, the Buggenum helmet started to replace the Montefortino pattern commonly worn by legionaries of Caesar's legions. On the neck guard of this bronze helmet are scratched two inscriptions, one above the other. The external (older) one reads: | • POSTVMI • M • VALERI • BACINI – Marcus Valerius Bacinus (or Bacenus) century of Postumus. The internal (newer) one reads: | • CAESIDIENI • C • TOMIVS – Caius Tomius century of Caesidienos. The helmet obviously served two legionaries (with Celtic *cognomina*, or family names), one after the other. (© Esther Carré)

Fused remains of an iron mail shirt (Saint-Germain-en-Laye, Musée d'archéologie nationale, inv. 71442) unearthed at Chalon-sur-Saône (*département* of Saône-et-Loire). Several Roman mail shirts, usually rolled up as here, have been recovered from rivers such as the Saône. The use of linked iron rings to forge a flexible form of body armour by the Romans stems from their having borrowed the idea from the Gauls. The latter had used them since the 3rd century BC, albeit reserved for the aristocratic warrior elites such as the Vachères warrior. Roman mail shirts came in two styles known according to the originators, the Gaulish and the Greek. During the last century of the Republic the first was very popular with horsemen; the second had shoulder reinforcements modelled after those of the Greek linen corselet, which provided extra protection against downward sword strokes. (© Esther Carré)

the legion needed to operate effectively. In Gaul the most prominent of these legates was Titus Atius Labienus, Caesar's second-in-command as a *legatus pro praetore* (*BG* 1.21.1), who at times was employed as an independent army commander. In theory, he could command the entire army in Caesar's absence. Still, Caesar states his conception of the legate's role in defending Publius Sulla from failing to pursue the Pompeians at Dyrrhachium (Durrës) in 48 BC. 'For the duties of a legate and of a commander are different: the one ought to do everything under direction, the other should take measures freely in the general interest' (*BC* 3.51.4, cf. *BG* 1.41.3). In other words, a legate was to obey orders; demonstrating initiative was not encouraged. Caesar chafed at independent action; it was the leader's prerogative to take sole control and direct the soldiers.

Obviously Caesar liked to play his chess without consulting the pieces. It is interesting to consider whether he regarded his flesh and blood legions purely as pawns. Needless to say, the appointment of legates by Caesar was a makeshift, the benefit of which was so apparent that it was adopted by Augustus as a permanent solution. Yet, the legates loom large in the military history of the late Republic, and many of them were first-rate soldiers of considerable experience. Such was Labienus, a military man from Picenum (Le Marche) who owed his career thus far to his service in Pompey's wars.

Another important factor in preserving collected experience and skill in the Roman army was the rise of the professional centurion. In a legion of Caesar's time there were 60 centurions, 6 in each of the 10 cohorts. The highest centurial rank was that of *primus pilus*, 'first spear', the chief centurion of the legion who nominally commanded the first century in the first cohort. Although Polybios comments on the care taken to select determined fighters to fill the ranks of the centurionate of his day, it is only in the late Republic that these men become more prominent. An example of the latter is Publius Sextius Baculus, *primus pilus* of the newly raised legio *XII*, who was seriously injured at the river Sabis (*BG* 2.25.3). In two other (later) instances during the civil war we find men like Marcus Cassius Scaeva, who received several serious wounds and lost an eye defending one of the *castella* (forts) at Dyrrhachium (*BC* 3.53.3–4), and Caius Crastinus, the former *primus pilus* of *legio X*, who died while leading the charge at Pharsalus (*BC* 3.99.2). These men are depicted as heroic figures, men who inspire the soldiers under their command through their conspicuous courage.

In his *commentarii* Caesar himself emerges as the all-conquering commander, but his centurions are the true heroes. They were a tough, hand-picked bunch of men of great dependability and courage. Referring to those celebrated rivals Titus Pullo and Lucius Vorenus, who vied with each other in exhibiting bravery, Caesar says these two were 'close to entering the *primi ordines*' (*BG* 5.44.1). The six centurions of the first cohort were collectively known as the *primi ordines*, 'front rankers', and enjoyed immense prestige. Centurions *primorum ordinum* were coupled by Caesar with the military tribunes and were regarded as members of the councils of war he regularly

8

held with his senior officers. Wise commanders recognized the value of their centurions not only in leading men into battle, but also in providing valuable advice based on their experience of war. Caesar himself would have listened to their views and used them to pass on information and orders to the rank and file. Their understanding of an intended battle plan was vital for success simply because they were the ones leading the men on the ground. Centurions were the key to an army's success in battle, and Caesar knew it.

During the Gallic campaigns Caesar's army more than doubled in size, creating many opportunities for promotion to higher grades of the centurionate. An army with a high percentage of new recruits (who tired and blistered easily) did not lend itself to conquest that easily. To counter this, Caesar closely associated veterans and rookies. He understood that it is only by the habits of soldiering, and after several campaigns, that the soldier acquires the moral courage that allows him to bear out the fatigues and privations of war without a murmur. In this way the veterans were a valuable asset to a new legion, having gained experience in soldiering and having been tempered and tested in actual combat. Thus, the ranks of newly raised legions were salted with a valuable cadre of experienced centurions promoted from junior grades in veteran units. These were men who could pass on their skills.

On several occasions Caesar notes that he promoted gallant centurions from lower grades in veteran legions to higher positions in recently raised units. Scaeva, mentioned above, was transferred from 'the eighth cohort to the post of first centurion of the first cohort' (*BC* 3.53.5), that is, *primus pilus*. The raw recruits of the newly minted *legio XIIII* were stiffened by, as Caesar writes, 'a number of centurions who, because of their bravery, had been transferred from the lower ranks of the other legions to the higher ranks of this' (*BG* 6.40.10). Such men included Baculus, also mentioned above,

Pectoral hooks (Saint-Germain-en-Laye, Musée d'archéologie nationale, inv. 50188, 50123) consisting of two S-shaped clasps and a central button. These come from an iron mail shirt found at Chassenard (*département* of Allier). While *pila* and *gladii* represent the mass-produced, mercantile aspects of war, pectoral hooks are more individual items. This fine example, from a soldier's burial dating to around AD 40, has snake-head terminals and bears the engraved inscription A · BLVCIVS · MVCI (Aulus Blucius Mucianus), which is perhaps the name of the wearer. (© Esther Carré)

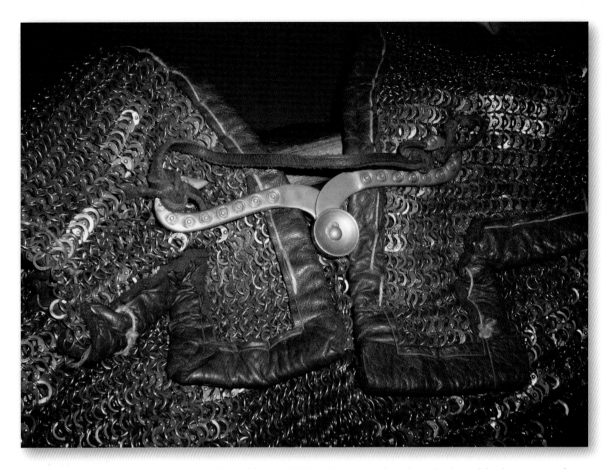

Full-scale reconstruction of pectoral hooks (MuséoParc Alésia) attached to the shoulder doubling of a re-enactor's well-made *lorica hamata*. (© Esther Carré)

primus pilus of *legio XIIII*, who, though sick in bed, grabbed weapons from the nearest soldiers and barred the entrance to the camp as it was about to be overrun by the Gauls (*BG* 6.38). The fearless Quintus Fulginius, one of the said legion's *primi ordines*, 'who by his remarkable valour had risen to that post from the lower rank of centurions' (*BC* 1.46.6), fell fighting outside the Iberian fortress of Ilerda (Lérida). Likewise, the courageous Marcus Petronius, a centurion of *legio VIII*, who refused to retreat from Gergovia despite death being close at hand, thereby allowing his men to escape; 'In this manner he soon afterwards fell fighting, and proved the saviour of his men' (*BG* 7.50.6). Petronius represents the ideal of the hard, but honourable, consummate centurion.

Unfortunately, however, we have no real clue to the selection of these officers and whether they entered the army as junior officers or were promoted from the ranks. What is clear is that once a man joined the centurionate, he became an individual of some status. Moreover, in time he often became a wealthy man from the booty he had acquired and the bonuses he had been paid. As well as promotion, Scaeva was also rewarded with a bounty of 50,000 denarii, a princely sum equivalent to well more than 200 years' pay for an ordinary ranker. Indeed, the booty from the Gallic campaigns was lavishly distributed amongst Caesar's soldiers, and conspicuous service was rewarded by decorations and rapid promotion. Little wonder they revered him.

OPPOSING PLANS

For the Gaul who had some experience of the invader's battle tactics, where the enormous weight and power of the armoured legionaries carved their wide paths through the packed mass of unarmoured tribesmen, the standing fight was not the route to success. A different kind of war was preferable, where tribesmen could suddenly emerge from their native forests and fens and fall upon isolated units of Romans, and by sheer surprise and strength do brisk butchery before flying as fast as they had fallen. To beat the invaders without a major battle, if we understand battle to mean a full-scale confrontation between armies, was the locals' trump card.

It stands to reason that a military nation and a warlike nation are not necessarily the same. The Romans were warlike from organization and instinct, and most of their accounts of the Gauls fit the conventional characterization of barbarians as ignorant, argumentative, stupid and volatile. They lie, break their oaths, are unpleasant and, worse still, in war they prefer ambush to stand-up encounters for which Rome's disciplined soldiers were specially trained and equipped. Whereas the Gauls were warlike, the Romans were militaristic.

A *caliga* (Saint-Germain-en-Laye, Musée d'archéologie nationale, inv. 2257) from the site of the legionary fortress at Mainz. The standard form of military footwear for Caesar's legionaries, *caligae* consisted of a fretwork upper, a thin insole and a thicker outer sole. The 20mm-thick outer sole was made up of several layers of cow or ox leather glued together and studded with conical iron hobnails. Weighing a little under 1kg, the one-piece upper was sewn up at the heel and laced up the centre of the foot and onto the top of the ankle with a leather thong, the open fretwork providing excellent ventilation that would reduce the possibility of blisters. It also permitted the wearer to wade through shallow water, because, unlike closed footwear that would become waterlogged, they dried quickly on the march. (© Esther Carré)

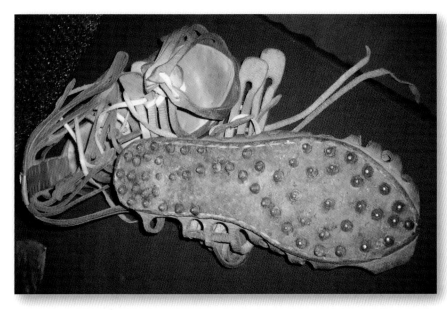

Evidence from Kalkriese, the probable site of the Varian disaster in AD 9, suggests 120 hobnails per boot, though the frequent finds of hobnails at the site of Alesia suggests half as many would suffice for Caesar's legionaries. (Below) Iron hobnails recovered from Alesia, and (right) a pair of reconstructed *caligae* (MuséoParc Alésia). The hobnails served to reinforce the *caligae*, to provide the wearer with better traction, and to allow him to inflict harm when stamping. Moreover, the actual nailing pattern on the sole was arranged ergonomically and optimized the transfer of weight between the different parts of the foot when placed on the ground. Experiments with modern reconstructions have demonstrated that, if properly fitted, the *caliga* is an excellent form of marching footwear, and can last for hundreds of kilometres. Much like all soldier's equipment past and present, *caligae* would have needed daily care and attention, such as the replacement of worn or lost hobnails or the cleaning and buffing of the fretwork upper. (Below and right © Esther Carré)

VERCINGETORIX'S PLAN

Initially Vercingetorix's strategy was to draw the Romans into pitched battle. Major engagements were fought at Vellaunodunum (Montargis), Cenabum (Orléans) and Noviodunum (of the Bituriges, probably near the site of Neuvy-sur-Barangeon) in central Gaul. After this series of reverses, Vercingetorix realized that in pitched battle he was unable to match the Romans, who were too well trained and disciplined to be beaten in open warfare. Moreover, it was useless to try and hold one *oppidum* after another. Therefore he decided on the one strategy that might have been successful, namely to starve the invaders by means of a scorched-earth policy. In this way they would be in the unhappy position of being master of no more than the ground they encamped on, procuring their supplies at the point of the sword, and having their convoys jeopardized or seized. Hungry and demoralized, they would be forced to turn back.

To this effect Vercingetorix summoned his supporters to an assembly 'and told them of the need to continue the war according to a different strategy to the one they had adopted until now' (*BG* 7.14.2). He carefully explained his policy of avoiding pitched battle and wearing down the Romans by denying them any form of sustenance. Supplies were to be centrally stored in defended locations where they would not fall into the hands of the enemy. Fields were to be cleared of grain and fodder; not a stalk was to be left standing. All villages and farms along Caesar's line of march, wherever his foragers might conceivably reach, were to be burnt to the ground. In addition, all *oppida*, except those rendered impregnable by reason of their position and fortifications, were to be burnt. 'If these proposals seemed harsh and severe,' he concluded, they needed to remember that it was far worse to have their children and wives dragged off into slavery, and themselves be killed – 'and that was sure to be their fate if they were defeated' (*BG* 7.14.10). These drastic measures 'received unanimous support' (*BG* 7.15.1).

Unfortunately, and probably understandably, the rebels could not, or would not, see that to be effective the work of incendiarism had to ruthlessly maintained. Vercingetorix had no means of compelling them to do this. As well as the possibility of making barren land from the Garunna to the Sequana rivers, Vercingetorix had a second string to his war bow, namely the potential to pursue guerrilla warfare. Having scorched the earth and destroyed their own homes and fields, the Gaulish rebels could take to the high hills and the tall timber with their mobile beasts and all else they could move. They would then carry on the struggle by ambush, cutting supply lines and constant harrying. Vigorously pursued, the use of guerrilla tactics, coupled with a mass uprising, would leave Caesar and his army fighting a wasting, cruel and unpredictable war. To succeed in this, the Gauls would need to be patient and show a singleness of purpose, enforced by a tight discipline. However, due to their individualist tribal traditions, this was not the Gaulish way.

CAESAR'S PLAN

There is no denying that Caesar was caught on the wrong foot at the close of 53 BC. He needed to regain the initiative, and fast. On the positive side, he had under his command ten steadfast legions. However, Caesar was presently enjoying the hibernal delights of Gallia Cisalpina – he had set out for Italy 'to hold assizes as arranged' (*BG* 7.1.1) – and his legions were hibernating far away in Gallia Comata.

For us to suggest therefore that Caesar had a plan would be wrong. On the contrary, Caesar was to react to a distant but dangerous uprising that had caught him totally unawares. The few remaining weeks of the year were anxious times for both Caesar and his legions. The *oppida* of Gaul must have buzzed with wild rumours and false reports. None of the Romans, from Caesar downwards, could have gained a clear view of the whole strategic situation. Nevertheless, when he got to hear of the rebellion, Caesar neither dithered nor moved with caution.

With hindsight, it seems clear that the classic survival policy of devastating his own country combined with guerrilla warfare would have been the wiser course of action for Vercingetorix. Nonetheless, his skill in controlling an unwieldy confederacy of tribal forces under aristocratic tribal leaders, both instilling fear and inspiring courage, caused Caesar great difficulties. The latter's deeply assertive nature, and his love of glory, could hardly fail to rise to Vercingetorix's challenge. In the event, by brilliant leadership, force of

Full-scale reconstruction of the Italic oval, semi-cylindrical body shield, conventionally known as the *scutum*, used by Caesar's legions (Taberna Marciana, Aquileia). The face of this one has been decorated with the unit's insignia, which either was done in applied panels or painted (see Tacitus *Historiae* 3.23.2). However, it is not clear whether the entire legion shared a common shield device, or whether each cohort was distinguished in some way, perhaps by colour. The necessity of unit identification by shield device may have arisen from Roman fighting Roman during the perennial civil wars of the late Republic. The stylized wing, thunderbolt and lightening flash design (the emblem of Iuppiter) is popular in modern reconstructions.
(© Esther Carré)

(Right) The well-preserved blade of a *gladius* (Saint-Germain-en-Laye, Musée d'archéologie nationale, inv. 49824) found at Trévoux (*département* of Ain). The blade has a length of 610mm including the handgrip, with the blade itself measuring 479mm. This sword belongs to the first of two models of *gladius*, the long-pointed 'Mainz' type. With its superb two-edged blade and lethal triangular point, legionaries were trained to thrust, not slash, with this particularly effective weapon; a short stab in the belly of an opponent was enough to incapacitate him. (Inset) A bronze chape or scabbard point formerly belonging to a *gladius* (Saint-Germain-en-Laye, musée d'archéologie nationale, inv. 14449) found at Mont-Chyprés, Lacroix-Saint-Ouen (*département* of Oise). (© Esther Carré)

arms and occasionally sheer luck, Caesar succeeded in stamping out the rebellion in a long and brutal action. This was to culminate in the siege of Alesia.

In short, Caesar was overconfident. But then why should he not be? He was a man at the height of his powers and energy. He commanded an army that had scored notable victories over the Gauls, and in the process had demonstrated remarkable resilience and prowess. Furthermore, it was loyal to him, and him alone. Caesar's army was a compact force because of a fiercely exclusive *esprit de corps* that bordered upon fanaticism.

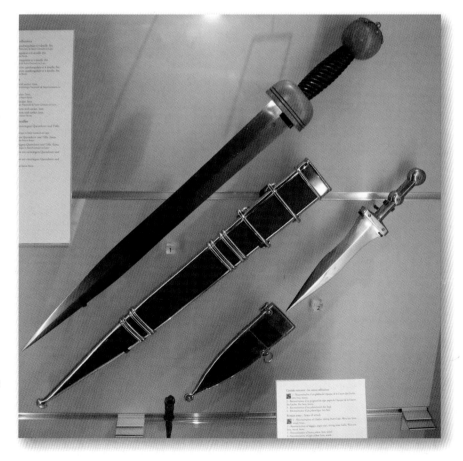

Full-scale reconstruction of a 'Mainz'-type *gladius*, the pattern carried by Caesar's legionaries, and a *pugio* or dagger (MuséoParc Alésia). The blade could be as much as 640 to 690mm in length and 48 to 60mm wide and waisted in the centre. It was a fine piece of 'blister steel', with a triangular point between 96 and 200mm long and honed down razor-sharp edges, designed to puncture armour. It had a comfortable bone handgrip grooved to fit the fingers, and a large spherical pommel, usually of wood or ivory, to help counterbalance the weight. Surviving examples weigh between 1.2 and 1.6kg. The *gladius* was carried high up on the right-hand side for ease of withdrawal and so not to expose the sword arm. In the press of a pitched battle, the legionary excelled in delivering the quick, sharp thrust. (© Esther Carré)

THE CAMPAIGN

The Gauls were made to believe this was the uprising that would see the destruction of their temporary masters, to hurl them back over the Alps. The opening offensive was against Cenabum (Orléans) in late 53 BC. After capturing the *oppidum*, the Carnutes slaughtered the entire Roman community there and took control of Caesar's major gain cache in Gaul. One of the most notable victims was Caius Fufius Cita, a merchant of equestrian status whom Caesar had placed in charge of the grain supply for his army (*BG* 7.3.1). It was Cenabum that gave the signal to the Gallic revolt. Caesar rushed over the Alps from Gallia Cisalpina, where he had been wintering, to his headquarters in Gallia Transalpina. However, he now found himself cut off from his legions in Gaul. Vercingetorix had shown his teeth.

Caesar's unexpected midwinter march across the snow-laden Mons Cevenna to threaten the heartland of the Arverni derailed Vercingetorix's plan, which was to start a widespread uprising in central and western Gaul before Caesar could rejoin his army after his usual winter visit to Gallia Cisalpina. Vercingetorix, swayed by the entreaties of his fellow Arverni, marched to the rescue. No sooner than he had arrived, Caesar, with a small escort of picked horsemen, started for his legions, and 'without breaking the march by day or night' (*BG* 7.9.4), kept ahead of news and peril and reached them safe and sound. He at once opened a winter campaign.

What was once the *oppidum* of Cenabum – *Kénabon* in Greek – the modern city of Orléans, looking across the Loire towards the Pont Georges V and the cathedral of Sainte-Croix d'Orléans, which is probably most famous for its association with Jeanne d'Arc. One of the chief strongholds of the Carnutes, Cenabum controlled a bridge over the Liger (Loire), and its strategic location on what was one of the four great west-flowing rivers of Gaul meant it served as the 'the emporium of the Carnutes' (*Geo.* 5.2.3). When Cenabum was occupied by Caesar in 54 BC, Roman merchants quickly established themselves there, including one Caius Fufius Cita, whom Caesar had installed to control commerce and ensure his army's grain supply. These corn brokers and traders, along with the small Roman garrison, were put to the sword by the Carnutes towards the end of 53 BC. Retaken and destroyed by Caesar in early 52 BC, Cenabum was largely rebuilt and re-fortified by the emperor Aurelianus in AD 273–74 and renamed *Aurelianum* or *Aureliana Civitas*, whence Orléans. (Patrick Giraud)

Caesar's campaign of 52 BC

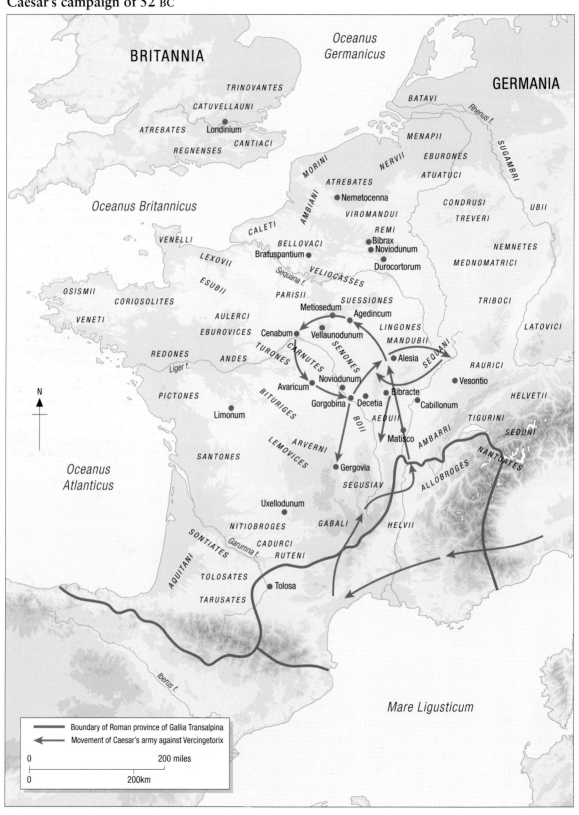

BRITANNIA

Oceanus Germanicus

GERMANIA

TRINOVANTES

CATUVELLAUNI

ATREBATES
Londinium

CANTIACI

REGNENSES

BATAVI

Rhenus f.

MENAPII

EBURONES

NERVII

ATUATUCI

SUGAMBRI

Oceanus Britannicus

MORINI

ATREBATES
Nemetocenna

CONDRUSI

TREVERI

UBII

AMBIANI

VIROMANDUI

VENELLI

CALETI

BELLOVACI

REMI
Bibrax
Noviodunum

NEMNETES

MEDNOMATRICI

LEXOVII

Bratuspantium

VELIOCASSES

Durocortorum

Sequana f.

OSISMII

CORIOSOLITES

ESUBII

PARISII

SUESSIONES

TRIBOCI

LATOVICI

VENETI

AULERCI

Metiosedum

Agedincum

LINGONES

MANDUBII

SEQUANI

REDONES

EBUROVICES

Cenabum

Vellaunodunum

SENONES

Alesia

RAURICI

Liger f.

ANDES

TURONES

CARNUTES

Vesontio

PICTONES

BITURIGES

Avaricum

Noviodunum

Bibracte

HELVETII

Limonum

Gorgobina

Decetia

Cabillonum

TIGURINI

SANTONES

LEMOVICES

ARVERNI

BOII

AEDUII

Matisco

AMBARRI

SEDUNI

NANTUATES

Gergovia

SEGUSIAV

ALLOBROGES

Oceanus Atlanticus

Uxellodunum

NITIOBROGES

GABALI

HELVII

SONTIATES

Garumna f.

CADURCI

RUTENI

AQUITANI

TOLOSATES

Tolosa

TARUSATES

Iberus f.

Mare Ligusticum

Boundary of Roman province of Gallia Transalpina

Movement of Caesar's army against Vercingetorix

| 0 | 200 miles |
| 0 | 200km |

N

The Gorges du Tarn, Cévennes – the mountain range known to the Gauls as Cebenna but Latinized by Caesar to Mons Cevenna or Cevenna (*BG* 7.8.2, 3, cf. *HN* 3.31, 4.17). Caesar crossed the Cévennes, probably in the middle of January 52 BC, in a bid to wrong-foot Vercingetorix by threatening his tribal homeland. Despite 6ft snowdrifts, not to mention the polar conditions, Caesar's hardy soldiers rose to the challenge and cleared a path through one of the passes to descend unchallenged upon the heartland of the Arverni. R. L. Stevenson's celebrated 120-mile solo tramp across the Cévennes took him, and his obstinate, manipulative donkey Modestine, 12 days. Setting out on 22 September 1878 armed with a notebook (and a revolver), Stevenson's hike became the subject of his *Travels with a Donkey in the Cévennes* (1879). Caesar's crossing, despite being executed when the Cévennes were solidly in winter's glacial grip, was undoubtedly done at a more cracking pace. He was only too well aware that speed was of the essence if he was to put Vercingetorix at a disadvantage. (Marek Ślusarczyk)

All the same, Cenabum proved to be only a *hors d'oeuvre* for a more substantial effort on the behalf of the Gauls, and there was worse to come for Caesar and his legions that year. As we know, Vercingetorix's initial strategy was to draw the Romans into pitched battle. However, after he was soundly beaten by Caesar in the open field at Noviodunum in the winter of 52 BC, he knew that in pitched battle he was unable to match the Romans, who were too well trained and disciplined to be beaten in open warfare by his fickle tribal levies. Taking advantage of the tribesmen's superior knowledge of their home territory, Vercingetorix thus began his canny policy of scorched earth, small war and defensive manoeuvres, which gravely hampered Caesar's movements by cutting off supplies for his army. For Caesar it was to be a grim year ahead. His whole Gallic enterprise faced liquidation.

In March of 52 BC Caesar moved quickly to eliminate one of the centres of resistance and so laid siege to the Biturgian *oppidum* of Avaricum. During the siege, the Gauls effectively used fortifications, fire and ballistics against Caesar's besieging legions. Despite the Gauls' attempts to lift the siege, the Romans ultimately cracked the fortifications and put to the sword Avaricum's inhabitants.

Roughly a month later, Caesar turned his attentions to the Arvernian *oppidum* of Gergovia. Vercingetorix, however, beat Caesar to Gergovia and, employing many of the tactics used at Avaricum, carefully prepared his defences. It was here that Vercingetorix came within a hair's breadth of beating the Romans, who lost almost 700 men including 46 centurions. Oddly Caesar, in his own testimony, claims he just managed to pull off a pyrrhic victory. This imposes in parts a severe strain on our credulity, and by reading between the lines we can suspect that, for the sake of prestige and moral, Caesar had waited until his Germanic horsemen had gained some minor victories before evacuating his position at Gergovia. Vercingetorix had given Caesar more than he had bargained for. Perhaps Caesar despised Vercingetorix, and so had underrated him. If so, Caesar knew better afterwards.

The modern city of Bourges, looking across the marshland towards the Gothic-style cathedral of Saint-Étienne de Bourges. Consecrated in 1324, the cathedral occupies what was once the north-eastern corner of the Gallo-Roman walled city. Originally this was the site of the fortified town of Avaricon, what Caesar calls Avaricum, 'a very large and well-fortified *oppidum* in the land of the Bituriges, and in a particularly fertile area of the territory' (*BG* 7.13.3). Despite Vercingetorix's sensible strategy of scorched earth, the Bituriges were reluctant to put the torch to Avaricum, which served as their tribal capital. They therefore opted to defend it. Sitting on a rocky prominence at the confluence of four rivers (today called the Yèvre, the Voiselle, the Auron and the Moulon), the *oppidum* was going to be a tough nut to crack for Caesar. This he did, and then proceeded to destroy it and slaughter most of its inhabitants. (Domenico Di Nolfo)

It is unclear why Vercingetorix was chosen to lead the rebellion in the first place, but the choice proved to be an inspired one. The young Arvernian war leader was by far the most able of Caesar's opponents, giving no end of difficulties until he was finally entrapped and besieged in Alesia. Before dealing in detail with the latter, however, more needs to be said about the two sieges of Avaricum and Gergovia.

THE SIEGE OF AVARICUM

The crossing of the Liger (Loire) by Caesar, and his march on Avaricum, drew Vercingetorix towards him. However, the Gaulish leader carefully avoided physical contact. He followed the Romans by easy stages and then encamped deep in a swampy forest, some 20km from the *oppidum*, presumably to entice Caesar into this unfamiliar, treacherous ground. If this was so, he was unsuccessful, for Caesar opened his operations against Avaricum without delay. The Bituriges were unwilling to sacrifice what was their chief *oppidum* by implementing the strategy of scorched earth advocated by Vercingetorix. Consequently, its 40,000 inhabitants opted to hold it against Caesar.

At Avaricum Caesar was obliged to construct an earthen ramp (*agger*) 80 Roman feet (23.67m) high, as the *oppidum* sat on moderately high ground amid impassable marshland at the confluence of four large rivers, what are called today the Yèvre, the Voiselle, the Auron and the Moulon. Consisting of earth and rubble with timber supports laid crisscross, this structure was completed in 25 days. The ramp's width of 330 Roman feet (97.6m) amply accommodated the two siege towers that gave the legionary working parties covering fire during the engineering phase. These working parties were

A scale model of the siege of Avaricum (West Point, Museum of the United States Military Academy). The *oppidum* was virtually surrounded by rivers and wetlands, but Caesar entrenched where there was a gap in the natural defences, a narrow approach along a ridge. In this scale model we see the earth and timber ramp (*agger*) up which the Romans pushed their two siege towers under the cover of a fierce storm. We also see the rows of end-to-end sheds (*vineae*) that had protected the legionary work parties during the engineering phase of the siege, and would then serve the same purpose for the legionary storming parties. Avaricum's fall would end in fire and massacre. (Rolf Müller)

protected by rows of end-to-end sheds (*vineae*). Vegetius (4.15) describes a *vinea* as a light timber structure, open-ended with wickerwork sides, a boarded roof and a fireproof covering of freshly flayed hides. Arranged end-to-end to form long corridors, these are perhaps the devices Caesar calls 'open tunnels' (*cuniculi aperti*). Behind the labouring work parties were the artillery – stone-throwing *ballistae* and bolt-shooting *scorpiones* – protected by a line of mantlets. The two siege towers were trundled up the ramp, the muscle power being provided by legionaries who were protected by side screens. However, the ramp was primarily designed to facilitate a mass infantry assault on the battlements.

The walls of Avaricum were constructed in the Gaulish style, what Caesar famously calls *murus gallicus* (*BG* 7.23.1). They comprised layers of stone alternated with heavy timber beams, these being laid in parallel lines, mortised or nailed together, with the interstices thus created being filled with compact earth or rubble. As he fully appreciated, this type of wall construction 'offers an excellent means for practical defence of cities. The stones gave protection from fire and the timber from battering rams – for it is impossible to break through continuous beams, usually 40 [Roman] feet [*pedes quadragenes*] long and secured on the inside, or to tear them apart' (*BG* 7.23.5). The whole circuit of the wall was studded with timber towers, furnished with fighting platforms and protected externally by dampened raw hides to thwart attacks by fire.

The Gauls were not content to conduct a passive defence, but skilfully harassed the besiegers with sorties and sabotage, and in this way countered every move the Romans made. As the Roman ramp approached and grew higher, providing the siege towers with greater height, they responded by extending upwards the fighting platforms within the facing towers, and frequently made sorties by day and night to ignite the Roman workings. When the Romans threw grappling irons on to the walls, the Gauls made them fast to windlasses and wound them up, human cargo and all. When the Romans erected scaling ladders, they cast them down. When the Romans constructed

The siege of Avaricum

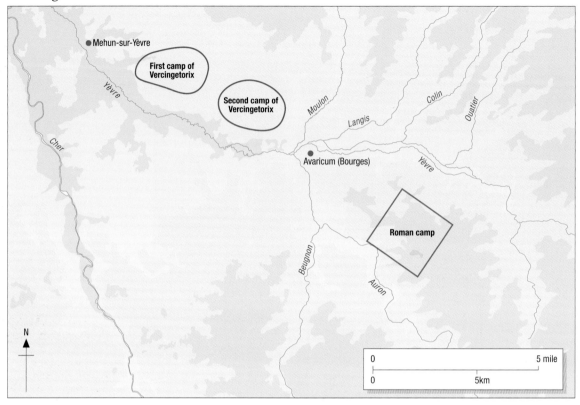

subterranean galleries (*cuniculi*) to enable attackers to approach the walls unseen and without danger, the Gauls countermined them from above, sabotaging further progress 'by the use of timbers tempered and sharpened at one end, boiling pitch, and heavy rocks' (*BG* 7.22.5). As Caesar sagely notes,

A section of the surviving circuit of the Camp Celtique de la Bure, Saint-Dié-des-Vosges (*département* of Vosges). The Gauls were prodigious fortification builders, and the *murus gallicus* was a peculiar Gaulish type of rampart. It had a wooden framework of intersecting heavy timber beams whose rows were separated by layers of compact earth or rubble. Mortising or long iron nails fixed the beams at each intersection. It was given a cladding of large blocks of close-fitting stone through which the ends of the beams protruded. Excavations at the western end of Mont-Auxois have demonstrated that the *oppidum* of Alesia had defences of the *murus gallicus* type. (Ji-Elle)

the Gauls, because of the extensive network of iron mines to be found in their country, were 'practised experts in every kind of tunnelling' (*BG* 7.22.2).

While all this was progressing, Vercingetorix had moved nearer to Avaricum. He had personally taken charge of the cavalry and those light-armed warriors who normally fought alongside the horsemen, in order to ambush Roman foraging parties. Caesar quickly took advantage of Vercingetorix's absence from his main camp, and slipped away from the siege lines before the *oppidum* at midnight to conduct a dawn assault upon the camp. The Gauls there, however, had been alerted and Caesar found them ready and waiting for his attack. Caesar returned to his siege lines. Vercingetorix also abandoned his mission without success and returned to find the tribes angry at his absence at such a crucial moment. Mutiny was clearly in the air, and they also complained that he had chosen a campsite too close to the enemy for comfort. Avaricum fell to Caesar a few days later.

Under the cover of a swirling rainstorm, Caesar ordered men to filter into the *vineae*. Emerging suddenly, the assault parties quickly scaled the walls with ladders and the less than diligent sentries were overwhelmed. The *oppidum* was soon lost, with only about 800 escaping death; Caesar claims that the inhabitants originally numbered 40,000 or thereabouts. Once over the walls, the legionaries had thrown themselves into an orgy of rape and pillage. Such were the excesses of victory.

A CLOSE-RUN THING: GERGOVIA

Unlike Avaricum, which Vercingetorix had not wanted to defend, Gergovia was one *oppidum* he did intend to hold, being as it was his tribal capital. It stood on an oblong plateau that crowned a hill rising to a height of 735m

The site of Gergovia, now Gergovie in the commune of La Roche-Blanche (*département* of Puy-de-Dôme). Excavations on this oblong-shaped plateau have revealed the fortifications of the *oppidum* as well as a large number of Italian wine amphorae of the Dressel IA type. The hill now known as La Roche-Blanche, where Caesar had planted his small camp, can be seen in the centre middle distance, with the route up to the col to the left. Gergovia was the chief stronghold of the Arverni, Vercingetorix's tribe. Here, in the spring of 52 BC, Caesar was to suffer a near defeat at the hands of this very capable 'barbarian' general. In the wake of the sanguinary encounter, Caesar, having lost nearly 700 men including 46 centurions, lifted his blockade of the Arvernian *oppidum* and eventually withdrew. (Frank Auvergne)

The siege of Gergovia

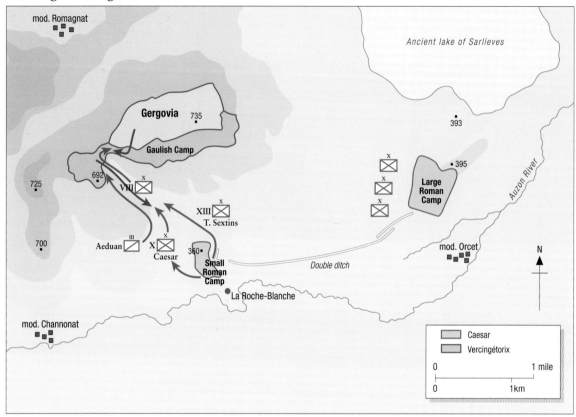

and dominating the surrounding plain. Its southern flank sloped in a series of terraces towards a 'hill at the foot of the plateau and sheer on every side' (*BG* 7.36.5), now called La Roche-Blanche, 1.5km south of and about 175m lower than Gergovia. Immediately beyond it flowed the Auzon river, a tributary of the Elaver (Allier), whose riverbanks provided lush pasture. This rock was the key to the defence of Gergovia and consequently Vercingetorix had garrisoned it.

From his reconnaissance it became apparent to Caesar that he could neither assault nor besiege the hilltop *oppidum*. He therefore decided 'to cut off the enemy's main water supply and prevent them from foraging freely' (*BG* 7.36.5). He thus encamped his army on a plateau some 3km to the south-east of Gergovia. A few days and another reconnaissance later it occurred to Caesar that if he were to occupy La Roche-Blanche, he would be in a position to cut his enemy off from part of his water supply and much of his forage. He had observed it was weakly held.

'In the dead of the night Caesar moved out of camp and expelled the garrison before it could receive reinforcements from the *oppidum*' (*BG* 7.36.7). Having taken La Roche-Blanche by a *coup de main*, Caesar did not intend to lose it the same way; another, smaller camp was erected and garrisoned by two of his six legions. From this he had his men dig two parallel ditches, each 12 Roman feet (3.55m) wide, to connect the small camp to the large camp. This allowed him to move his forces from one camp to the other without interference from enemy sorties. The next step was to capture

Eroberung Alesias duruch Cäsar (1533), oil on panel (Munich, Alte Pinakothek) by Melchior Feselen (d. 1538), a historical painter from Passau. Feselen's vivid composition of the siege of Alesia features a great number of figures (note the colourful *landsknechts* in their full fighting finery). The viewer is also offered a rich, albeit fanciful, rendering of Caesar's siegeworks. In his seventh *commentarius* Caesar never employs the terms contravallation or circumvallation. These terms first appeared during the epoch of Napoleon III. (© Bridgeman Art Library)

another hill much closer to the *oppidum*, which was immediately to its west and connected with it by a col. This hill is now known as Hauteurs de Risolles.

However, before this could be achieved, disturbing events elsewhere were to take Caesar away from Gergovia. He had received news that the north-eastern Gaulish tribe of the Aedui were becoming disaffected. Without further ado, he set forth in marching order with all his cavalry and four legions, aiming to bring the tribe to heel. He left his bags and baggage behind in the large camp together with his two other legions under the command of the legate Caius Fabius. Caesar, never a man to sit idly by, dealt swiftly with his recalcitrant allies and turned for Gergovia. When well on his way back, he was met by a galloper with the news that Vercingetorix had assaulted the large camp in full force; many men 'had been wounded by a hail of arrows

The iron 'business end' of a (below) *dolabra* found in one of the V-shaped ditches of Camp B, and (above) a reconstructed one (MuséoParc Alésia). The *dolabra* was the very versatile Roman version of what we know as a pickaxe. Throughout history, there has been a contemptuous aversion of soldiers to spadework. Nonetheless, at Alesia Caesar harnessed one of the Roman army's great strengths: engineering skills that were mobilized and organized to a single purpose. Each legion was perfectly capable of construction work because its ranks were well supplied not only with unskilled muscle but with skilled artisans too. Thus it was that Caesar's legions dug the complex of ditches and ramparts, and raised the parapet and intervening towers. (Below and above © Esther Carré)

and missiles of all kinds' (*BG* 7.41.3). On account of the size of the camp – it had been constructed to accommodate six legions, not two – the defenders had been hard pressed to satisfactorily man its ramparts. Fortunately for them, however, the artillery (*tormenta*) had broken the Gaulish assault. By a supreme effort of his men, Caesar reached Gergovia before sunrise.

On a visit to the small camp, Caesar noticed that the Hauteurs de Risolles – the hill hard by the *oppidum* – which had previously been crowded with Gaulish warriors now appeared to be undefended. Interrogating some deserters, he found out that Vercingetorix feared that, should the hill be lost, he would be cut off from all egress to forage; as a result, he was fortifying it. Caesar decided to draw the bulk of the Gauls out of the *oppidum* by means of a feint attack on the southern flank of the hill, and then launch a frontal assault from his small camp against Gergovia via the col.

The Gauls had thrown up 'a six-foot wall of large stones' (*BG* 7.46.3) halfway up the hillside. Caesar's feigned build-up of his troops opposite the southern flank of the hill included a number of muleteers mounted on their mules and wearing helmets so as to resemble cavalry. This ruse worked, forcing Vercingetorix to shift a large body of warriors to the hill so as to defend it against this apparent threat, leaving their camps virtually empty.

In the meantime, Caesar led his men from the large camp to the small one by way of the route defended by the double ditches. Then out of the small camp he unexpectedly launched three legions (*VIII*, *X* and *XIII*) against the

wall, which was virtually unguarded while the Nitiobroges (a tribe of south-western Gaul) who had been posted there were resting. The legionaries quickly crossed the wall, and seized three camps so unexpectedly that Teutomatus, the king of the Nitiobroges, was forced to flee from his tent 'half-naked on a wounded horse' (*BG* 7.46.5). The jubilant legionaries pressed on until they neared the walls of Gergovia, a few of them even scaling them and entering the *oppidum*. Their jubilance was to be short lived. The bulk of Vercingetorix's army was soon shifted back to the Gaulish camps, and a pitched battle ensued. Tired and disorganized, the Romans were driven from the camps and bundled down the hillside.

There was at least one factor that should have caused Caesar to act with less haste. The Romans had a weakness, and it was a fairly substantial one: having previously achieved victory with ease, they believed they were right and clever. This helped blind the Romans to the nature of the forces they had helped to unleash.

Indeed, like Goethe's sorcerer's apprentice, they had conjured up forces they could not control. In this respect, Caesar was to fall victim to his own prejudices and pigeonholing.

As Caesar regrouped his army, he would have realized the day had not gone well for him; almost 700 of his men were dead and, worse, amongst them were 46 of his centurions. The Gauls, one suspects, must have seen him off with joyful celebration. Rather than admit failure at Gergovia, Caesar blamed the over-enthusiasm and disobedience of his men (*BG* 7.52, cf. 45.7–8, 47.2–4), and he pretended to be satisfied with the capture of three half-empty Gaulish camps (*BG* 7.46.4–47.1). So goes Caesar's version. However, even the dullest-witted legionary was probably coming to realize that the current campaign in Gaul was not going well for his side.

Was this lapse of discipline an exceptional case caused, as Caesar claims, by the passions of the moment? Or did it betray other, more fundamental shortcomings, like an institutionalized ardour that bordered on recklessness? Although Caesar's genius is often shown when extracting his army from a difficult situation with sword in hand, he may be accused of foolhardiness for allowing the situation to materialize in the first place. At Gergovia, as he was to do again at Dyrrhachium, Caesar snatched a result from a situation full of peril. This turning of the tables on his enemies was achieved by rapidity of movement and force of personality.

NOVIODUNUM

Having struck camp, Caesar moved into the territory of the Aedui. When he came to the river Elaver (Allier), he bridged and crossed it. The Aedui, until recently ardent supporters of Rome, had raised the flag of rebellion and declared their allegiance to Vercingetorix.

Noviodunum (close to Nevers), an Aeduan *oppidum* situated on the river Liger, was Caesar's administrative base. Here were to be found all his Gaulish

A full-scale section of Caesar's siegeworks, reconstructed at the Archéodrome de Beaune, Merceuil (*département* of Côte-d'Or). Such a double-line of investment was familiar Hellenistic practice, but Caesar's bi-circumvallation has always attracted particular admiration. Here we see the camouflaged pitfalls (*lilia*), beyond which lie the double ditches and earthwork (reconstructed in concrete) crowned with a breastwork of timber. Sharpened forked branches (*cervi*) are embedded in the earthwork, while timber towers overlook the defences. According to Caesar's testimony the original inner ring of defences (contravallation, designed to prevent the Gauls leaving Alesia) ran for 11 Roman miles (16.3km), with a corresponding outer ring (circumvallation, designed to keep out enemy reinforcements) of 14 Roman miles (20.7km). (Christophe Finot)

A full-scale section of Caesar's siegeworks, contravallation and circumvallation, measuring around 100m in length have been erected outside the Interpretation Centre, MuséoParc Alésia. At the time of photographing, it was being repaired after suffering damage during heavy rain, and needed to be provided once more with a battlement parapet wall with a narrow walkway behind it. Nonetheless, even in this impaired condition we get a good impression of what Caesar's men threw up around Mont-Auxois. Though much less impressive than the example at Beaune, which was fabricated by following the drawings commissioned by Napoleon III, the breastwork and towers are in all likelihood more realistic. (© Esther Carré)

hostages, his grain reserve, his war chest, remounts for his cavalry and the best part of the army baggage. Eporedorix and Viridomarus, two young chieftains of the Aedui, turned on the Roman garrison at Noviodunum and slaughtered them together with the traders gathered there, released the hostages, divided the money, carried away as much grain as they could transport and dumped the remainder in the river, and torched the *oppidum*. Gathering local recruits, the two young Aeduans picketed the Liger and sent out mounted raids in the hope of disrupting Caesar's line of communications and forcing him to retreat into Gallia Transalpina. The situation was looking bleaker for Caesar.

Did he see fit to retreat to the relative safety of the south? The answer was an emphatic 'no'. Instead, he took the bolder course and struck out northwards so as to link up with Labienus, who had just concluded a successful campaign against the Parisii and Senones. By forced marches, day and night, he reached the Liger so speedily that the Aedui were taken off-guard. He crossed the swollen river via a deep ford, halted for a brief spell to gather in cereal and cattle and then marched into the territory of the Senones in order to reach Labienus' base camp at Agedincum (Sens). With a reunited army, Caesar now sought to regain the initiative.

On re-establishing contact with the Romans, Vercingetorix risked a cavalry fight, perhaps hoping that the destruction of Caesar's mounted arm would hinder his ability to monitor Gaulish movements and make foraging harder. However, the Gauls were routed, Caesar's new levies from across the Rhenus proving their worth. In this modest battle, Caesar's Germanic horse sustained the shock of Vercingetorix's mounted attack. The Gaul recoiled to the *oppidum* of Alesia to recover and replenish his cavalry, which were both thinned in numbers and demoralized in spirit. As Caesar says, Alesia was 'an *oppidum* of the Mandubii' (*BG* 7.68.1), a client tribe of their powerful neighbours to the south, the Aedui. The stage was now set for a final showdown in the Gaulish rebellion.

THE FINAL ACT: ALESIA

To understand the siege conducted by the Romans against Alesia, one must first visualize the countryside in which they operated. The *oppidum* of Alesia sat atop a mesa-like hill (Mont-Auxois, 407m), its plateau (97ha/239.69 acres) falling off precipitously, plunging perpendicularly for a third of its 150m height. It is roughly of an oval form, running east to west for about 1,500m and north to south for 600m. Alesia itself covered only the western end of the plateau, where the hill sloped very steeply, the eastern end accommodating Vercingetorix's camp. Mont-Auxois itself was part of a much larger limestone plateau, which had been eroded by two rivers running east to west north and south of the hill, the Oze and the Ozerain, both tributaries of the Brenne. These left two deep valleys, which separated Mont-Auxois from the surrounding hills of Mont-Réa (375m), Montagne de Bussy (422m), Mont-Pennevelle (403m) and Montagne de Flavigny (430m). To the west of Mont-Auxois the two river valleys merged to form a broad plain, the Plaine des Laumes, which was dominated by a string of roundtop hills, the Collines de Mussy-la-fosse (408m), and watered by the Brenne.

The nature of Roman operations was dictated by these physical realities. To make matters more difficult for the enemy, Vercingetorix had 'constructed a ditch and a six-foot wall' (*BG* 7.69.5), probably of rough unhewn stone, where Mont-Auxois faced east; this made an approach to his camp from that most accessible quarter almost as difficult an assault. With his 80,000 warriors (*BG* 7.71.3, 77.8) and 15,000 horsemen (*BG* 7.64.1), which seem remarkably high figures, the star-crossed Vercingetorix believed Alesia was unassailable.

It was at Alesia, if anywhere, that Caesar displayed his true military genius for the first time. Although outnumbered, Caesar was not to be outgeneralled. Commanding fewer than 50,000 legionaries and assorted auxiliaries,

LEFT
The double V-shaped ditches that form part of the reconstructed section of the contravallation at the MuséoParc Alésia. The Gauls would have crossed these on a causeway of fascines and brushwood. Though these are filled to the brim with water (the result of heavy rain), the inner ditch was a dry one (on the right), and thus the attacking Gauls would have passed over it dry-shod.
(© Esther Carré)

RIGHT
The river Brenne, looking upstream at Camping Alésia, Venarey-Les Laumes. This picture was taken in October when the water level is on the rise, reaching its yearly maximum in the month of February (15.60m³/s). However, during the summer months the river has a meagre discharge, falling as low as 1.69m³/s in August. In truth, it does not provide much of an obstacle.
(© Esther Carré)

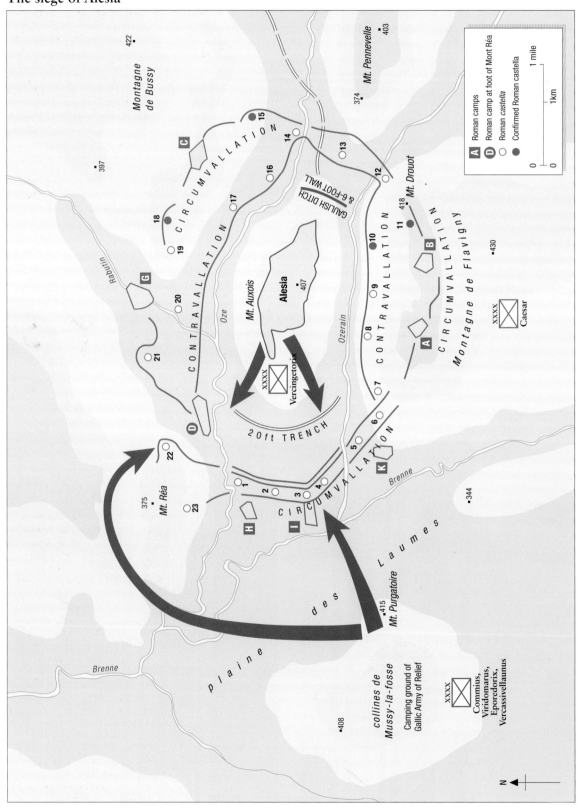

The river Ozerain, looking downstream from the Pont de Laizan (which carries the D10 to Flavigny-sur-Ozerain). As can be seen from this photograph, which was taken in the month of October, the Ozerain was easily fordable. Its waters and those of the Oze were dammed and diverted so as to flood the outer ditch of the contravallation. Consequently, in the summer months when the river was much lower, we have reason to conclude that it became a rivulet, which a man might easily jump over. (© Esther Carré)

he began a regular siege without delay. This he did by ordering Mont-Auxois to be encircled with extensive siegeworks, the object being to entrap Vercingetorix, cut off all communication and provision, and effectively localize the rebellion. What might earlier have seemed to Vercingetorix like an impregnable position capable of defeating any assault made upon it had become a trap. However, as soon as the danger of an investment was apprehended, and before the Roman siege ring could close around him, Vercingetorix dispatched his cavalry to rally reinforcements from across Gaul.

Contravallation and circumvallation

In turn, Caesar decided to upgrade his siegeworks. Rather than a series of all-out assaults on Alesia, he had chosen to strangle and starve the Gauls into submission. Caesar improved his works into a bi-circumvallation – two lines of investment instead of one – so as to cut Vercingetorix off from all external succour. On completion, one line (the contravallation) would face and

The river Oze, looking upstream towards the Pont des Romains. Caesar tells us that the foot of the hill upon which Alesia perched was 'washed by two rivers' (BG 7.69.2). Those French archaeologists and historians who are profoundly uneasy about the identification of Alesia with Alise-Sainte-Reine point out, among other details, that the Oze and the Ozerain are not rivers (flumina, in Caesar's Latin) but little streams. The 'Jurassics', as the dissenters are known, are convinced that the original excavations at Alise-Sainte-Reine were deliberately falsified. However, according to authority and orthodoxy, they rely far too heavily on their interpretation of Caesar's words. (Phil25)

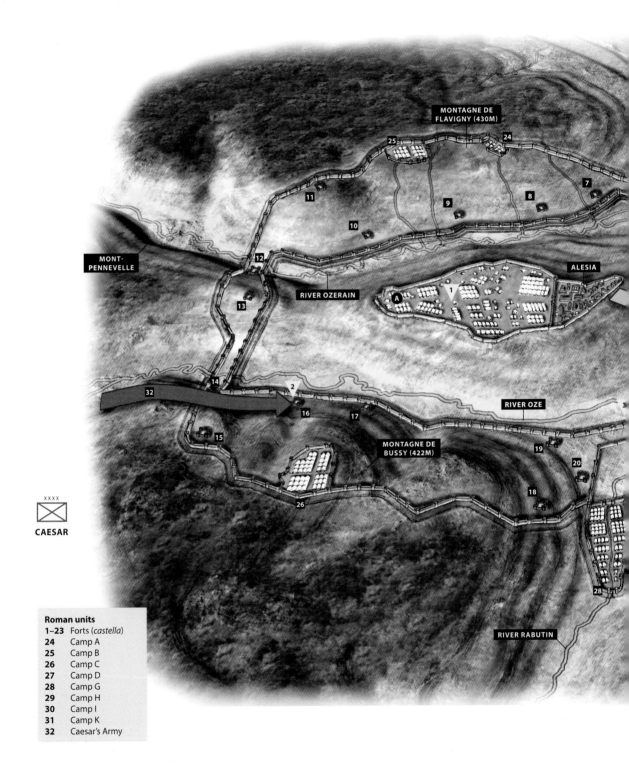

MONTAGNE DE
FLAVIGNY (430M)

MONT-
PENNEVELLE

RIVER OZERAIN

ALESIA

RIVER OZE

MONTAGNE DE
BUSSY (422M)

RIVER RABUTIN

XXXX

CAESAR

Roman units
1–23 Forts (*castella*)
24 Camp A
25 Camp B
26 Camp C
27 Camp D
28 Camp G
29 Camp H
30 Camp I
31 Camp K
32 Caesar's Army

THE SIEGE OF ALESIA

Caesar decides to invest Alesia and Vercingetorix's camp, as the Gaulish leader calls upon other tribes to lend help.

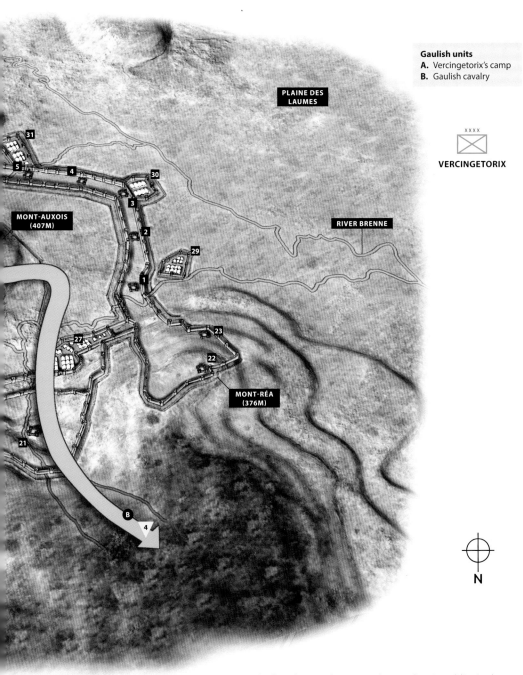

Gaulish units
A. Vercingetorix's camp
B. Gaulish cavalry

x x x x

VERCINGETORIX

PLAINE DES LAUMES

MONT-AUXOIS
(407M)

RIVER BRENNE

MONT-RÉA
(376M)

N

EVENTS

1. Vercingetorix and his rebel army of many tribes (80,000 foot warriors and 15,000 horse warriors, according to Caesar) retire to Alesia (Alise-Sainte-Reine), a well-girt *oppidum* of the Mandubii near the source of the Sequana (Seine). Alesia itself occupies the western end of Mont-Auxois (407m), an oval mesa-like hill between the rivers Oze and Ozerain, both tributaries of the Brenne. The flat top of the hill falls off on steep sides, and the *oppidum* walls form an extension of the hillside. Vercingetorix's camp occupies the eastern end of the same hill, the approaches to which he protects with a ditch and wall.

2. Commanding fewer than 50,000 legionaries and assorted auxiliaries, Caesar judges an assault to be unworkable, and so decides to invest Alesia and Vercingetorix's camp. Mont-Auxois is encircled by hills of similar height, control of which is essential if Caesar is to maintain a tight grip on his anticipated siege operations. He establishes seven or eight camps around Alesia, such as camps A and B on Montagne de Flavigny (430m), the hill south of Mont-Auxois, and Camp C on Montagne de Bussy (422m), the hill 1.5km north-east of Mont-Auxois.

3. Caesar invests Alesia by throwing up an elaborate contravallation 11 Roman miles long to keep Vercingetorix bottled up within, and a circumvallation 14 Roman miles long as a defensive line against any relief forces without. The engineering work includes

damming and diverting the waters of the Oze and the Ozerain so as to flood the outer of the two ditches of the contravallation. In addition, to slow the approach of any daylight assault and to disrupt any night sorties mounted by the besieged Gauls, the Romans devise more elaborate obstacles, such as *lilies* and *cippi*, today known as *trous de loup* and *abattis*.

4. Before the Romans can complete their siegeworks – they will take around a month to do so – Vercingetorix, already worried by supply shortages, sends out his horsemen by night. He has ordered them to proceed to their prospective tribes and urges them to come to his assistance with all possible speed. If the siege goes on for too long, Caesar could easily find himself fighting back Gaulish relief attacks while attempting to keep the lid on Alesia.

53

Caesar's siegeworks were supplemented by an ingenious arrangement of obstacles including *cippi*, *stimuli* and *lilia*. (Below) Circular pits, *lilia*, just in front of the Antonine Wall fort of Rough Castle, Falkirk. These pits were so called by the Roman soldiers because of a resemblance to the lily with its vertical stem and enclosing leaves. Arranged in checkerboard configuration, these pitfalls once contained sharpened, smooth stakes cunningly camouflaged with twigs and foliage. (Right) The *lilia* at MuséoParc Alésia, part of the reconstructed section of the circumvallation. These were not necessarily meant to kill, but they were designed to wound and slow or halt the enemy, the point of penetration being the foot or calf. (Below and right © Esther Carré)

encircle the hill, while the other (the circumvallation) would face away from the hill and encircle the contravallation.

There exists a certain degree of confusion over the use of these two terms. Tellingly, Caesar does not use the words contravallation and circumvallation in his seventh *commentarius*. However, in his very brief description of the siege of Vellaunodunum he does use the technical verb form of *circumvallavit*, 'encircled it with entrenchments' (*BG* 7.11.1). The terms first appear in publications concerning Alesia in the epoch of Napoleon III – in French *contrevallation* and *circonvallation* – terminology that was in all probability first coined by Vauban (1633–1707). The Union commander Major-General Henry Wager Halleck (1815–72) provides a clear and concise explanation in his *Elements of Military Art and Science*: 'The works thrown up between the camp and besieged place are termed the *line of countervallation*, and those on the exterior side of the camp form the *line of circumvallation*.' (1862: chapter XIV, 'Field-engineering')

Caesar's elaborate system of investment at Alesia was far from unique in classical history. Three instances from the epoch of Greek city-state wars will be sufficient to exemplify this point. Thucydides describes how the Peloponnesians during the summer of 429 BC, finding that they were getting nowhere outside Plataia, 'began to make preparations to throw a wall about it' (2.77.1) and then 'proceeded to throw a wall around the city' (2.78.1). Again, Thucydides describes how the Athenians besieging Mytilene in the summer of 428 BC 'fortified two camps, one on each side of the city, and instituted a blockade of both harbours' (3.6.1). Thirdly, Xenophon tells us that in the summer of 385 BC Agesipolis of Sparta, wishing to invest Mantineia,

Two iron *stimuli* (MuséoParc Alésia). Originally each of these thin, barbed iron spikes would have been firmly embedded in two wooden stakes, now long perished thanks to the effects of nature. The Latin name is of course ironic, as a *stimulus*, a spur, was designed to increase speed rather than, as here, forcing a halt. The *stimulus*, by means of its stake, was firmly hammered into the ground so that only the point protruded; when stood upon, the spike would be driven through the foot. The barbs prevented easy extraction, with the unfortunate having to tear his foot clear, leaving a nasty wound. (© Esther Carré)

ordered half of his army 'to build a wall round the city' (*Hellenika* 5.2.4). It is interesting to note that before Plataia was invested by the Peloponnesians, the Athenians, marching to the city, supplied food and a small garrison, 'taking way the least efficient of the men along with the women and children' (Thucydides 2.6.4). A sensible precaution indeed, one perhaps Vercingetorix should himself have done at Alesia.

Caesar may have also drawn inspiration from Roman history, notably Scipio Aemilianus' siege of Numantia in 134–133 BC. Appian (*Iberica* 15.90–1) tells us that the circumference of Numantia was some 24 stades (*c*.4.5km), while the Roman siegeworks around the town ran for a total distance of 48 stades (*c*.9km). The latter consisted of a stone wall 8 *pódes* (2.4m) wide and 10 *pódes* (3m) high 'exclusive of the parapet', with timber towers at intervals

Aerial view from the west of the picturesque village of Alise-Sainte-Reine (*département* of Côte-d'Or), formerly the site of Alesia. The oval-shaped plateau of limestone is Mont-Auxois, and it is this feature that Caesar surrounded with his extraordinarily complex siegeworks. The latter took about a month to complete. Archaeological examination, both on the ground and from the air, has indicated that the double lines of investment were not as complete as Caesar suggests. There may have been gaps in the siege lines, particularly where the terrain provided natural protection. The valley in the centre is that of the Ozerain, with Montagne de Flavigny rising in the background. (© Réne Goguey)

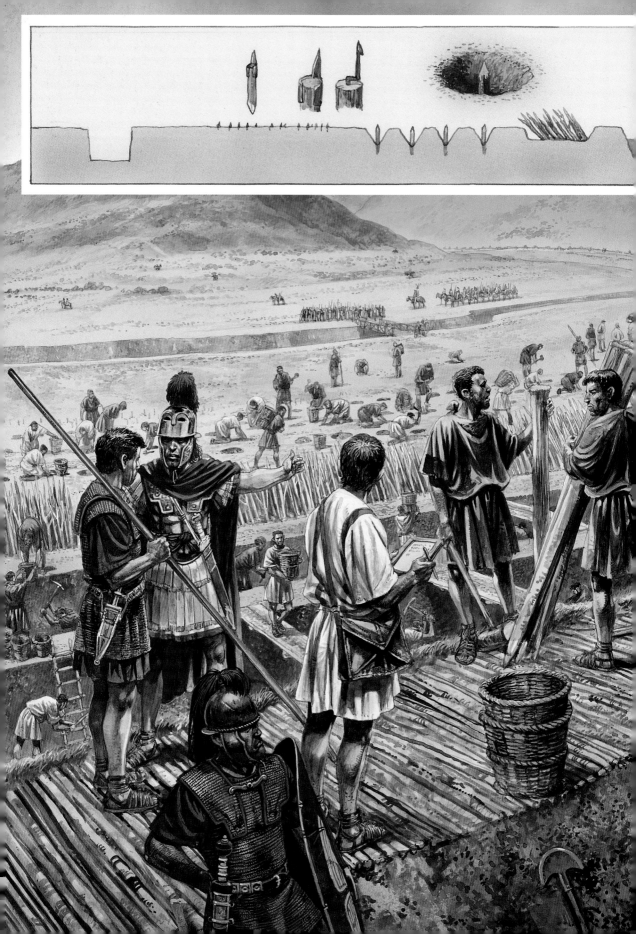

THE ROMAN SIEGEWORKS AT ALESIA (PP. 56–57)

We have a good idea of the lines of investment dug and erected around Alesia as Caesar's detailed description of it has been corroborated by the work of French (and more recently German) archaeologists. The excavations and topographical surveys were begun at the instigation of Napoleon III (under the direction of the indefatigable Colonel Baron Stoffel), and continue to this day with the additional benefits of aerial photography and magnetic survey. Though Caesar's account gives the impression that his siegeworks were more extensive than the current evidence suggests, his men were certainly experts in the art of moving earth. This artist's reconstruction shows the Roman engineering operations in full swing around Alesia.

The legionaries have piled up their arms and armour, being stripped down to their tunics and military belts (**1**). Other legionaries in fighting order act as sentries. We also see one of Caesar's legates on a tour of inspection (**2**); he is busy discussing matters with a centurion (**3**). The legate is accompanied by a legionary, ox-broad and black-browed, who serves as his bodyguard (**4**); he is in fighting order minus the *pilum*. The centurion is holding what was known as a *decempedae*, a rod 10 (Roman) feet in length (**5**). Vegetius, in a passage describing what he calls a *castra stativa*, stationary camp, says that during the construction of the ditch and rampart the 'centurions measure the work with ten-foot rods, to check that no one through laziness has dug less than his share or gone off line' (Vegetius 3.8). Caesar's men may have carried 'a palisaded camp in their packs', but like all armies there were no doubt shirkers and slackers skulking in the ranks.

In the insert we see the detailed construction of the obstacles – the *lilia* (**6**), *stimuli* (**7**) and *cippi* (**8**). The intention was that they should impede the enemy advance in any way possible.

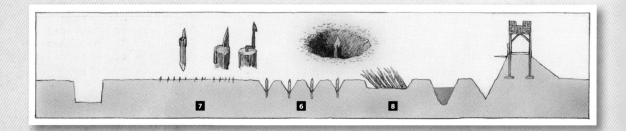

Mont-Auxois (407m), upon which the *oppidum* of Alesia perched, looking south-east from the D103. As it was built on top of an inaccessible cliff, Vercingetorix believed Alesia was secure. Though Alesia's position was one of great natural strength, he was quite wrong. Now thickly covered with deciduous trees (the result of modern reforestation), in Caesar's day Mont-Auxois had a treeless top, and its abrupt, sheer-sided limestone plateau would have been clearly visible. This bold height where steep slopes protected against an all-out assault – the *oppidum* walls would have been a vertical extension of the sheer part of the hillside – gave no such security against starvation. So Caesar turned to the latter, which after three months proved successful.
(© Esther Carré)

of a *plethron* (30.85m) and a V-section ditch 10 *pódes* (2.96m) deep on the Numantine side. Seven camps were placed around the perimeter, while the Duero, a nearby river, was blocked by a boom consisting of tree-trunks bristling with knives and spearheads. Appian's account is corroborated by archaeological remains of the Roman siegeworks still surviving on the bleak hillsides around Numantia.

According to Caesar's own words, the bi-circumvallation stretched for a total of 25 Roman miles, or 37km (*BG* 7.72), connecting with more than 50 Roman miles (74km) of ditches, numerous observation towers (a figure of 1,500 or so has been suggested) and breastworks, and linking an encircling chain of 23 redoubts (*castella*) on the forward slopes (to limit the Gauls' freedom of movement) and eight large camps (*castra*) on the surrounding hills and flats (to accommodate the siege army).

Whether or not one chooses to believe such impressive dimensions (and it has been postulated that Camp I is in fact post-Roman), the engineering works themselves were certainly elaborate. They consisted of a sheer-sided

Montagne de Flavigny (430m), the hill immediately south of Mont-Auxois, looking south-south-east from the MuséoParc Alésia. This is the location of Camp A (408m) and of Camp B (425m). Camp A was the smallest of the camps, covering 2.3ha (5.68 acres) and shaped like a haricot bean. Situated at the western end of Montagne de Flavigny, its position offered a good view of the Plaine des Laumes. No enemy could approach unseen. It had two gateways (north and south), the south gateway being protected by the double V-shaped ditches of the circumvallation. It was in this camp that a sizeable goatskin leather fragment from the corner of a *contubernium* tent was found. Camp B was 7.3ha (18.04 acres) in size and the excavation work there has revealed its outer facing rampart was studded every 7m with four-posted timber observation towers measuring about 3m x 3m in area, a probable indicator that the camp stood in a dangerous sector of the circumvallation.
(© Esther Carré)

(Right) Montagne de Bussy, looking north-east from Mont-Auxois. The three Roman camps on plateaus were constructed upon very hard, but at the same time very fractured, limestone; this made it an excellent construction material. Camp C, located on the crest of Montagne de Bussy (422m), the hill 1.5km north-east of Mont-Auxois, is the best known of Caesar's eight camps thanks to meticulous excavation and aerial photography (the work of Réne Goguey). (Below) An aerial view of Camp C taken from the south. It was 6.9ha (17.05 acres) in size; three of its gateways (north-east, east and south) have been discovered so far. (Right – ©Esther Carré; Below – ©Réne Goguey)

trench 20 Roman feet (5.92m) wide across the broad Plaine des Laumes, situated at the western foot of the hill; it served to protect the men working on the contravallation 400 Roman paces (592m) behind this, and faced inwards towards Mont-Auxois (1 pace or *passus* equalled 5 Roman feet or *pedes*; 1 Roman foot or *pes* equalled 296mm). This engineering work consisted of two V-shaped ditches each 15 Roman feet (4.44m) wide and 8 Roman feet (2.37m) deep; the two local rivers, the Oze and the Ozerain, were dammed and diverted to carry water where possible into the outer ditch. These broad ditches were covered by an earth and turf rampart and a palisade of planks or hurdles, 12 Roman feet (3.55m) in overall height and studded with timber observation towers every 80 Roman feet (23.67m). Forked branches were firmly embedded in the top of the earthwork so they projected horizontally, preventing any attempt to scale it. Sharpened and directed outwards, Caesar calls them *cervi* ('stags'), an ancient form of barbed wire.

Model of the north-east gateway of Camp C (MuséoParc Alésia). The gateway had a 10m-wide passage marked by a break in the V-shaped ditches of the circumvallation and was equipped with a two-leafed gate protected by a *titulus* (a mound and ditch) and *clavicula* (a rampart extension). The weakest point of a Roman camp, the gateway could receive additional protection from a *titulus*, which was built several metres to its front, or a *clavicula* that curved either outwards or inwards. Excavations have demonstrated that the north-east gateway was protected by both systems – the *titulus* can be seen here – which meant its *clavicula* curved inwards. Additional protection was provided by a double row of *cippi* (sharpened stakes). (© Esther Carré)

This brisk itinerary conveys little if nothing of the challenges which the legionaries faced in turning their commander's orders into reality. Just the preparation phase alone would have involved such back-breaking tasks as clearing the surrounding countryside to a billiard-table nakedness and logging local timber. An inkling of the colossal amount of physical labour involved can be derived from experimental archaeology. At the Lunt, a 1st-century AD Roman turf and timber fort near Baginton, Warwickshire, a team of Royal Engineers reconstructed a length of a turf-revetted rampart with a basal width of 5.4m and a height of 3.6m to the walkway. It was calculated that to build the total length of the rampart with one-third earth fill, a circuit measuring some 283m, would require the cutting of 138,000 standard-size turf-blocks. Vegetius (3.8) specifies the optimum size of such turf-blocks, 1.5 by 1.0 by 0.5 Roman feet (444 x 296 x 148mm), but it is not known if the legionaries at Alesia cut turf to a standard size. If they did, a turf-block would have weighed about 30kg, though the weight is largely irrelevant as the load was determined not by weight but by size. The experimental work by the Royal Engineers, and pre-mechanization military manuals and estimators' handbooks, all suggest a work-rate of around ten minutes for cutting a single turf. With a labour force of 210 to 300 men, working ten hours per day under good weather conditions, the rampart could be completed, along with a double-ditch system, in nine to twelve days. For the purpose of discussion, we will here propose that a 300m stretch of Caesar's contravallation (minus its timber towers and palisade) would have taken 300 legionaries around ten days to complete. What that figure meant in terms of human effort and application is worth a moment of reflection.

To slow the approach of any daylight assault and to disrupt any night sortie mounted by the besieged Gauls, the Romans devised more elaborate obstacles; camouflaged circular pits in a checkerboard formation concealing sharpened, smooth stakes, what would now be known as *trous de loup* but ironically nicknamed by the legionaries *lilia* ('lilies'). In front of these were scattered *stimuli* ('spurs'), short wooden stakes with barbed iron spikes embedded in them. Dug in the earth in the form of an inverted truncated cone, the *lilia* were just deep enough to ensure that the weight of a careless step would drive the stakes right up through the foot and out of the instep or straight through the fleshy calf, producing a nasty wound. As for the barbed iron spikes, it would have taken much time and pain to free any impaled victim.

Between these vicious booby traps and the two ditches were *cippi* ('gravestones'), five rows of branches, their ends lopped off and sharpened, fixed in channels 5 Roman feet (1.48m) deep and interlaced to form a hedge of vicious spikes, much like an *abattis*. As Polybios had earlier said of these, 'it is impossible to insert the hand and grasp them, owing to the closeness of the interlacing of the branches and the way they lie upon one another, and because the main branches are also carefully cut so as to have sharp ends' (18.18.13). Obviously, the longer the enemy was held in check by these obstacles, the longer he was exposed to the missile fire of the main work.

It is worth pausing to differentiate between field fortifications and those of a permanent nature. The main difference between properly constructed permanent fortifications (intended to resist a siege) and temporary works (usually of an earthen nature) is that the latter seldom present an insuperable obstacle against assault, while the former always do. For the besieged, sorties should have been frequently repeated, in order to interfere with and prolong the siege operations being conducted. The best time for making such sorties would have been an hour or two before daylight, when the enemy's guards were sorely fatigued with the labours of the night. Caesar mentions only one

Mont-Drouot (418m), looking south-south-east from the D103, the minor road that runs along the southern foot of Mont-Auxois. Mont-Drouot, a spur at the eastern end of Montagne de Flavigny, is the location of Castellum 11. This was possibly home to a couple of Caesar's cohorts, their parent legion in all probability being part of the garrison of Camp B, which was close by on the main crest. (© Esther Carré)

Mont-Pennevelle (403m), looking east-south-east from Mont-Auxois. Mont-Auxois is connected via a small col to Mont-Pennevelle, a ridge that points like a finger towards its eastern end. As this col provided the easiest approach route up and onto the plateau, Vercingetorix had his men construct a ditch and wall, the latter being 6 Roman feet high in Caesar's estimation, at this end of Mont-Auxois. (© Esther Carré)

such sortie mounted by the Gauls trapped in Alesia, but we can assume that Vercingetorix was not lax in this way. His men probably made frequent nightly attempts to harass the besiegers and to retard the construction of their contravallation.

As alluded to earlier, Caesar was clearly concerned about the likelihood of attack by other Gauls, which Vercingetorix was contriving to organize. As a result, he ordered his already fatigued men to construct a parallel line of defences as a circumvallation to ward off a likely Gallic army of relief. The bane of any legionary's life must surely have been digging, and Caesar's men spent more time wielding an axe or a pick than they did shouldering a *pilum* or drawing a *gladius*. Yet there was still the prospect of bloodshed and slaughter, and Caesar knew full well that he could bind his men for the coming trial with sweat and grind. Perhaps it would not be too much to assert that Caesar let his men grouch and complain, for it would have made them feel

Plaine des Laumes, looking south-south-west from the MuséoParc Alésia. Just to the west of Mont-Auxois is the Plaine des Laumes, an alluvial, open plain over 3km in length through which the Brenne meanders and meets its tributaries the Ozerain and the Oze. In the mid-1st century BC, low, scrubby vegetation would have covered the plain, broken only by the rude tracks that passed for roads in that part of the world. The Franco-German excavations on this plain have indicated that the circumvallation was fronted by a 3.5m-wide ditch, then an 8m gap, and finally a 5.7m-wide ditch. Obstacles were planted not only beyond the ditches but between them too. (© Esther Carré)

THE BESIEGED GAULS MOUNT A NIGHT-TIME SORTIE (PP. 64–65)

Though Caesar only records one night-time sortie, which was mounted against 'the lines of defences in the plain' (*BG* 7.81.1), we can conjecture that before the arrival of the army of relief Vercingetorix had not idled the summer away. Sorties would have been mounted against the siegeworks not only to disrupt progress during the building phase, but also to test the defences once they were completed.

The Gauls had become more sophisticated in their methods of siege warfare, and in this artist's reconstruction we see them armed with fascines, scaling ladders, poles and grappling irons, for crossing the ditches and mounting the rampart (**1**). Some are even carrying what Caesar calls *musculi*, 'sheds'. Being portable, these were probably heavy wickerwork shields, similar in size and design to the medieval pavise, for protection against Roman arrows and missiles (**2**). The time most favourable for a surprise was usually an hour or two before daybreak, as at this moment the sentinels were generally less vigilant, and those not on duty in a profound sleep. Moreover, any subsequent operations, after the initial surprise, would be facilitated by the approach of day.

However, the Gaulish assault was rendered more difficult because of the darkness. In the confused fighting that ensued

along the contravallation, many missiles were exchanged in the dark. In his retelling of the nocturnal sortie in the Plaine des Laumes, Caesar implies that casualties were caused on both sides by forces firing on their own troops by mistake. Today we call such tragic accidents 'friendly fire' or, much more befittingly, 'blue on blue'.

In this reconstruction it is the dead of night and the Gauls besieged in Alesia have mounted a full-scale assault upon Caesar's contravallation. Having negotiated the pitfalls and traps (designed to slow them down and keep them exposed longer to the lethal hail of missiles from the main work), the attackers have filled the inner ditch with fascines and are scaling the Roman ramparts (**3**). A bloody hand-to-hand tussle is about to take place over the wicker breastwork. From their battlements and towers, the defenders are hurling and dropping a multitude of missiles and whatever else they can lay their hands on to spoil the Gaulish assault (**4**). Understandably, in times of dire need – such as now – anything would be used. The Romans are also firing *scorpiones* at point-blank range, which are mounted on the timber observation towers (**5**).

like soldiers not slaves. Likewise, he must have let them joke too, for none would fear and laugh at the same time. Though it fatigued the body, it was no doubt helpful to keep busy, rather than to dwell on the coming battle; an engagement promised death and mutilations for thousands. There was a downside to all this extra labour, however. Even though it gave maximum defensive strength, the circumvallation potentially allowed the besiegers to become besieged themselves. This was, indeed, what came to pass.

A commander worth his salt has to prepare for any number of contingencies simultaneously. Knowing is half the battle. No doubt Caesar sat late into the night in his command tent (the *praetorium*) in the centre of one of the camps, poring over his maps and wondering just exactly what kind of relief force he would face.

When the Gallic army of relief did arrive, the Romans faced the warriors in Alesia plus an alleged 250,000 warriors and 8,000 horsemen attacking from without, according to Caesar's record. A quarter of a million is a dubious figure for the Gaulish forces, and Caesar could have inflated the number to make the main battle more dramatic. Even so, plainly outmatched numerically the Romans certainly were, and for the soldiers themselves the army of relief must have been a fearful thing to gaze upon. As for Caesar, though he now faced overwhelming odds, he was not to be easily intimidated. A commander whose *métier* was to take risks, the gambler's mentality was not lacking in him. Besides, despite their initial fears, his legionaries would be in their element, engaging in a head-on contest against warriors that would surely conduct a direct charge. The fate of Alesia would be decided by

The Collines de Mussy-la-fosse (408m), looking south-west from Mont-Auxois. These are the heights that rise above the western border of the Plaine des Laumes. It was somewhere here that the Gallic army of relief encamped before sweeping down to its destruction. To their left is Mont-Purgatoire (415m), a spur ending in a conical-shaped hill. (© Esther Carré)

Mont-Réa (375m), looking north-north-east from MuséoParc Alésia. This is a hill north-west of Mont-Auxois, at the foot of which squatted Camp D. Caesar simply refers to this vital spot as 'a northern hill' (*septentrionibus collis*, *BG* 7.83.2). On the final day of the main battle this hill was the location of some of the most savage fighting between the Gauls and Romans. (© Esther Carré)

'hand strokes'. The legionaries knew from experience that military success depended upon other factors, such as their state of training, unit cohesiveness and, above all, their ferocious military discipline, rather than upon sheer numbers.

Battle commences

In common with many battles of the ancient world, the evolution of the ensuing main encounter at Alesia cannot be precisely reconstructed. On the first day the army of relief paraded their great strength on the Plaine des Laumes, the horsemen to the front and the warriors a short distance behind. It made a brave showing. Meanwhile, Vercingetorix led his men down from Alesia and began to fill in stretches of the sheer-sided trench that ran across the plain. All was set for attacks from both directions. The plan was a good one and it might have worked. However, Caesar adroitly made maximum use of his interior lines, his fortifications and the greater training and discipline of his men to offset the Gallic advantage. Moreover, once again Caesar's Germanic horsemen proved their superiority over their Gaulish counterparts.

There was no fighting on the following day, as the Gauls made proper preparations to cross the ditches and scale the ramparts. And so it was that at midnight the relieving Gauls paid the enemy the compliment of imitation. Having equipped themselves with fascines (sticks bundled together for filling in the ditches), scaling ladders (the most common, though hazardous, means of entry), poles, grappling irons and what Caesar calls *musculi*, 'sheds' (*BG* 7.84.1, cf. 81.1, *BC* 2.10, Vegetius 4.16), they attempted to breach the circumvallation across the Plaine des Laumes. The noise of their assault heralded their arrival to Vercingetorix, who sent his own men into battle. In the darkness a brutal and confused fight ensued. Two of Caesar's legates,

A full-scale reconstruction of a four-posted timber observation tower, MuséoParc Alésia. The Romans were aware of the varied characteristics of different species of tree. Analysis of waterlogged twigs, branches and charcoal recovered from the ditches of Camp A on Montagne de Flavigny has revealed the sorts of timber they used in their construction work. Tree species included alder, beech, hornbeam, linden, oak, poplar, maple and willow. It is difficult to calculate the total acreage of wood exploited by the Romans, but Caesar says 'he placed towers all round the siegeworks at intervals of 80 Roman feet' (23.67m, *BG* 7.72.4). From this statement it has been estimated that Caesar's men logged some 6,000 trees so as to construct the 1,500-plus observation towers that studded the bi-circumvallation investing Alesia. In practical terms, this represents a deforestation of about 60ha (148.26 acres) of forested land. (© Esther Carré)

Marcus Antonius and Caius Trebonius, 'took men from towers further away and sent them to assist as reinforcements where they realised that our men were under pressure' (*BG* 7.81.6). Both of the Gaulish assaults were eventually repelled.

Before dawn the Gauls set out to capture the north-western angle of the circumvallation (Mont-Réa), which formed a crucial point in the Roman siegeworks. A picked force under the Avernian Vercassivellaunus – 60,000 strong, according to Caesar (*BG* 7.83.4) – moved forward and 'he concealed himself beyond the mountain [Mont-Réa] and ordered his soldiers to rest and recover from their efforts of the previous night' (*BG* 7.83.7). At midday the assault went in.

Caesar's indispensable lieutenant Titus Labienus took part in the fierce fight that followed, particularly around the camp of the legates Caius Antistius Reginus and Caius Caninius Rebilius (Camp D), which turned out to be unfavourably situated on a gentle downward slope. The Gauls had got

MONTAGNE DE FLAVIGNY (430M)

MONT-PENNEVELLE

RIVER OZERAIN

ALESIA

RIVER OZE

MONTAGNE DE BUSSY (422M)

RIVER RABUTIN

XXXX

CAESAR

Roman units
1–23	Forts (castella)
24	Camp A
25	Camp B
26	Camp C
27	Camp D
28	Camp G
29	Camp H
30	Camp I
31	Camp K
32	Labienus with six cohorts

THE SIEGE OF ALESIA

The Roman besiegers become besieged as the Gaulish relieving force arrives en masse.

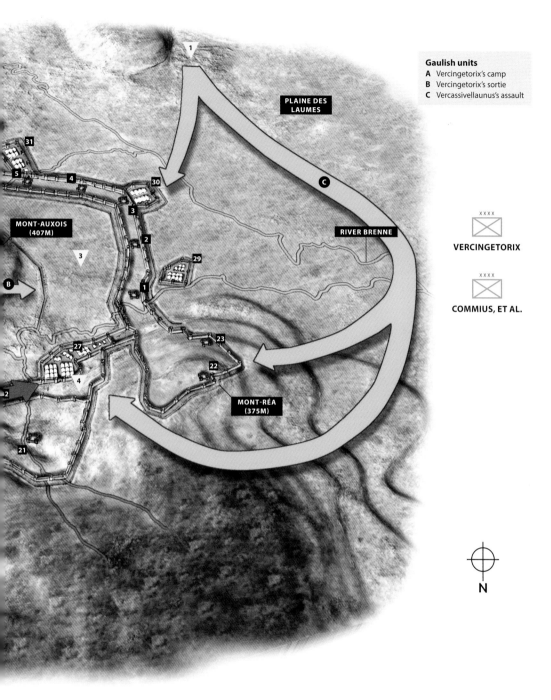

Gaulish units
A Vercingetorix's camp
B Vercingetorix's sortie
C Vercassivellaunus's assault

PLAINE DES LAUMES

MONT-AUXOIS (407M)

RIVER BRENNE

MONT-RÉA (375M)

VERCINGETORIX

COMMIUS, ET AL.

N

EVENTS

1. Vercingetorix has not been idle, hindering the Roman construction work by mounting sorties. However, he has not succeeded in preventing the completion of the bi-circumvallation. Eventually, a sizeable Gaulish relieving force (which Caesar claims consists of 250,000 foot warriors and 8,000 horse warriors) led by four war leaders, Commius, Viridomarus, Eporedorix and Vercassivellaunus, comes to the rescue of Vercingetorix.

2. The Gallic army of relief establishes its cantonment on the Collines de Mussy-la-fosse (408m), a string of round-top hills that rise above the western border of the Plaine des Laumes, the open plain just to the west of Mont-Auxois. Having already gathered all available forage in the near vicinity, Caesar continues his siege of Alesia despite the break out and relief attempts by the Gauls within and without.

3. After a clash between opposing horsemen – Caesar's Germanic horse once again proving their worth – the relief army mounts two major assaults. Vercingetorix organizes simultaneous sorties out of Alesia in support. The second, more serious assault is directed against the circumvallation across the Plaine des Laumes, the Gauls having now equipped themselves with the necessary paraphernalia for breaching the Roman defences. The Romans with great difficulty manage to beat back all assaults.

4. On the final day a picked Gaulish force under Vercassivellaunus (60,000-strong according to Caesar) is sent off before dawn against a crucial point of the circumvallation. The assault goes in at midday. The heaviest attacks fall upon the vulnerable Camp D, which is situated on the gentle slopes of Mont-Réa (375m), the hill to the north-west of Mont-Auxois. Caesar dispatches Labienus at the head of six cohorts to strengthen the two legions already there under the legates Antistius and Caninius. The hand-to-hand fighting in this threatened sector of the circumvallation is intense

(Below) Iron boltheads from a Roman *scorpio*, a light bolt-shooter, and (right) a full-scale reconstruction of a *scorpio* (MuséoParc Alésia). According to Vitruvius (*DA* 10.10), one of Caesar's mechanical experts, a three-span machine was a popular size, combining as it did portability with power. Such a machine shot a bolt three times a hand span, which was equivalent in length to 27 Roman inches (690mm), and was served by a two-man crew. A long-range, hard-hitting, efficient and deadly accurate weapon, during the siege of Avaricum Caesar describes the terrifying power and precision of the *scorpio* (*BG* 7.25.2–4). The boltheads are the usual pyramid-shape and (see reconstruction below, top) would have tipped an ash shaft with three wooden flights. (Below and right © Esther Carré).

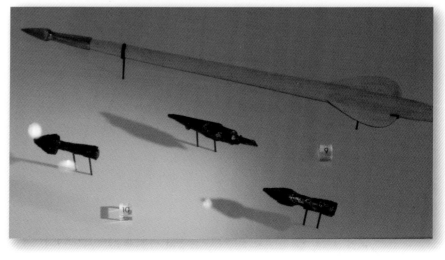

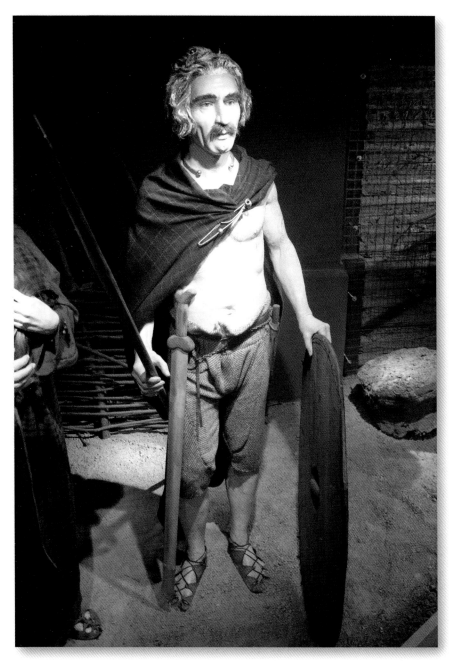

A life-size manikin of an attrited Celtic warrior (Kraków, Muzeum Archeologiczne). When thinking of the Gaulish warriors who fought and died at Alesia, one should not imagine they were all equipped *à la* Vachères warrior. Nor were they as young and virile. Uniformity was never a characteristic of any tribal war band, and the quality and quantity of weapons and equipment would vary widely, ranging from the abundant to the minimal. With the exception of all but a few wealthy warriors, body armour was not worn and the existence of metal helmets rare. Men of fewer means, the warrior farmers who formed the military backbone of war bands, were without armour and were almost certainly armed with a shield for protection, a spear for thrusting and a sword for slashing. (Silar)

to within hand-to-hand range and the camp was in danger of giving way when Labienus punched through with six cohorts. His orders were to hold as long as possible and then, as a last resort, draw his troops from the walls and sally forth (*BG* 7.86.1–2). The Gauls must surely have felt they were having the best of the battle – as indeed they were – and that at last they were on the verge of making an end of Caesar and his siege army.

The final battle was a struggle on such a scale – sweeping so many men into its swirling midst – that it is all too easy to forget that several significant events were happening simultaneously. While Labienus, Antistius and Caninius were fighting for their lives, Caesar himself was winning the battle

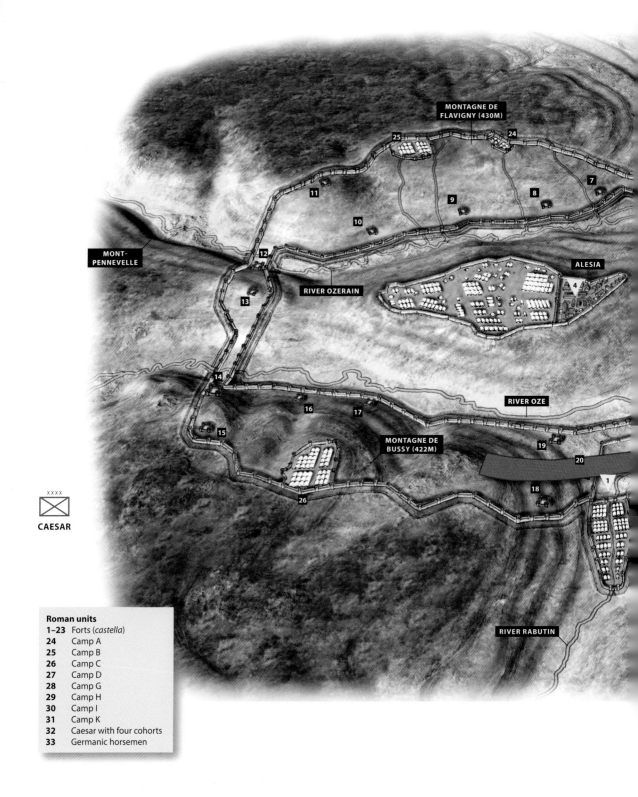

MONTAGNE DE FLAVIGNY (430M)

MONT-PENNEVELLE

RIVER OZERAIN

ALESIA

RIVER OZE

MONTAGNE DE BUSSY (422M)

RIVER RABUTIN

CAESAR

Roman units
1–23 Forts (*castella*)
24 Camp A
25 Camp B
26 Camp C
27 Camp D
28 Camp G
29 Camp H
30 Camp I
31 Camp K
32 Caesar with four cohorts
33 Germanic horsemen

THE SIEGE OF ALESIA

Cesar's Germanic cavalry rout the Gaulish relief force, as the Roman leader takes personal command in the fighting at Camp D.

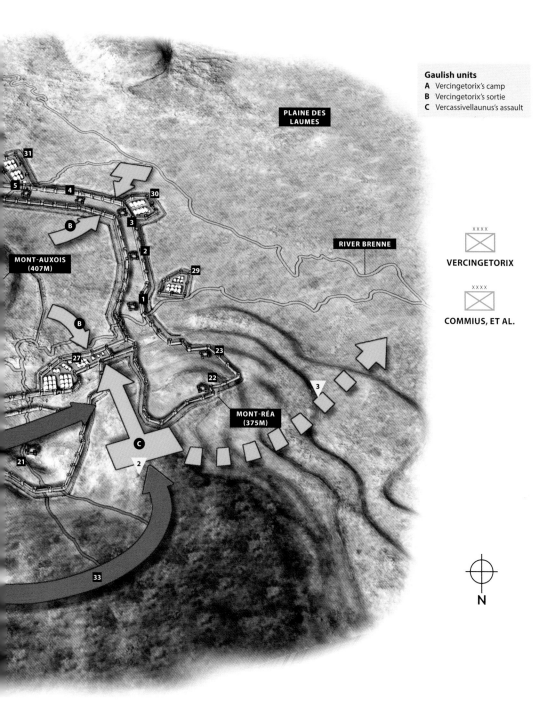

Gaulish units
A Vercingetorix's camp
B Vercingetorix's sortie
C Vercassivellaunus's assault

PLAINE DES LAUMES

RIVER BRENNE

MONT-AUXOIS (407M)

MONT-RÉA (375M)

xxxx
VERCINGETORIX

xxxx
COMMIUS, ET AL.

N

EVENTS

1. With the defences of Camp D on the brink of collapse, Caesar leads in person his very last reserve of infantry (four cohorts) in an attempt to turn back the Gaulish onslaught. The Gauls sense that triumph will be theirs. In the meantime, Caesar's Germanic horsemen unostentatiously exit the Roman siege lines by one of the gateways situated away from the fighting, preparing to strike the Gauls in the rear.

2. The conflict in and about Camp D reaches its climactic conclusion. The Gauls are heavily engaged at the crumbling ramparts, the Romans steeling themselves for a final effort to repel them once and for all, or die in the attempt. The Germanic horsemen make their surprise appearance out of the brown haze, and the Gauls are taken from the rear. The battle decisively turns to Caesar's advantage and the main Gaulish attack starts to unravel.

3. The Gauls turn tail, and the pursuing horsemen do their terrible work. Vercassivellaunus is taken alive and the spoils include 74 Gaulish war standards. Decisively shattered, the Gallic army of relief disperses. The survivors flee, making off to their various tribes.

4. Food supplies in Alesia have virtually disappeared, despite the fact that Vercingetorix had earlier expelled all the 'useless mouths'. With Alesia on the brink of starvation, Vercingetorix eventually capitulates to Caesar and becomes his captive. With the fall of Alesia, the effective resistance to Caesar in Gaul is checked.

Larger-than-life manikins depicting a well-armed Gaulish warrior fighting a Roman centurion (note his Montefortino helmet adorned with a *crista traversa*) at the time of Alesia, in the Combat Gallery, MuséoParc Alésia. Although the Gaulish warriors and Roman legionaries who fought at Alesia were ordinary people, they experienced extraordinary emotions and exhibited extraordinary behaviour in the midst of battle. (© Esther Carré)

everywhere except at the camp, or so he says. It was at what we know as Camp D that the day would be decided.

A message came from Labienus saying that the rampart and ditch were no longer defensible, and that with an additional 11 cohorts from the neighbouring *castella* (redoubts), he was going to break out. In all probability the general opinion among the Gauls was that the day would be theirs.

In desperation, Caesar cobbled together the last of his reserves and personally led them towards the thick of the fighting in a do-or-die counterattack. At the same time he dispatched cavalry (in all likelihood his Germanic horse and their loping foot warriors) around the circumvallation to come upon the enemy from behind (*BG* 7.87.2, cf. *HR* 40.40.4). His scarlet cloak signalled his arrival; in choosing this garment, Caesar showed his skills as a propagandist and his full awareness of the power of imagery. Like Alexander with his silvery war helmet flaming in the sun, and other subsequent imitators, he created an unforgettable image. His choice was more than simple vanity; he had a sure sense of what made effective military leadership and what gave an army identity and *esprit de corps*. He intended to be as conspicuous as possible, especially on the field of battle, both to his own men and to the enemy. He was Caesar, and his arrival had an enervating effect upon his weary men.

It was a near thing, even then. Whilst the Roman soldiers found new heart, the Gauls likewise renewed their efforts and zestfully threw themselves at the Roman defences again. The battle became more fierce. Caesar's men 'threw their *pila*, then fought with *gladii*' (*BG* 7.88.2). At this moment, the Germanic horsemen (and their unflagging foot warriors) appeared at the Gauls' rear and did their terrible work. The battle decisively turned to Caesar's advantage. The Gauls began to turn away from the fight, their minds now fixed on survival rather than victory. Panic set in, and many were cut down in flight. 'Only a few of the vast enemy host made their way safely back to camp' (*BG* 7.88.4). Caesar's memoirs make fairly light work of it, but the defenders of Camp D, thinned out by casualties and numb with fatigue, must have gazed over their battlements down the gentle slope of brooding Mont-Réa, thickly strewn with the terrible dead. The mighty Gallic army of relief, which at Vercingetorix's summons had come from across the face of Gaul, had been repulsed. The days were numbered for those besieged in the *oppidum*.

Food supplies in Alesia were almost exhausted, and useless mouths (belonging to the client tribe of the Mandubii, in the main) were taken off the ration list. Eventually, Vercingetorix had all the women, children, old and sick expelled, perhaps a preferable alternative to the slaughter and cannibalism that had been proposed by Critognatus, a member of his war council (*BG* 7.77; interestingly, his counsel to Vercingetorix is the longest direct speech recorded in the *commentarii*). The wretched outcasts begged to be accepted as Roman slaves and fed as such. However, Caesar recounts, with brutal clarity, that he forced them to stay at the base of the hill,

Vercingetorix jette ses armes aux pieds de Jules César (1899), oil on canvas (Puy-en-Velay, Musée Crozatier) by Lionel-Noël Royer (1852–1926). Caesar in his seventh *commentarius* paints a very restrained portrait of this episode (*BG* 7.89.4). Plutarch (*Caes.* 27.5; cf. *Epit.* 1.45.26, and *HR* 40.41.1–2) greatly improves upon the drama, with Vercingetorix donning his finest armour and having his horse carefully groomed. The Gaul rides high and handsome to the victor's camp, to eventually circle the enthroned Caesar before leaping from his horse to fall at his feet. Vercingetorix is still venerated and romanticized by the French public, and for some he has even donned the mantle of the ideal 'lost cause' hero, a political persona as protean as Jeanne d'Arc. This painting perhaps represents an inspired story rather than remembered history. (© Bridgeman Art Library)

THE FINAL GAULISH ASSAULT ON THE SIEGE LINES (PP. 78–79)

The last attack on the Roman lines of investment, which was made simultaneously from within and without, was to be decided by cavalry action. If we were privileged enough to have a bird's-eye view of Alesia, we would see the siege like a nest of boxes. In the centre is the wall-girt *oppidum*. To protect his camp without, Vercingetorix had fortified the eastern approaches to the limestone plateau. About Mont-Auxois Caesar had thrown up a bi-circumvallation, now being attacked by the Gallic army of relief from beyond. The latter is about to be surprised by the appearance of Caesar's Germanic horsemen (and their attendant foot warriors) behind its rear.

In this artist's reconstruction we see the situation at the height of the battle. We are witnessing the climax of the last attack, and Victory has suspended the scales between the combatants. In the foreground, Romans and Gauls are fiercely locked in a vicious hand-to-hand struggle over the Roman defences (**1**), while Caesar, as a final bold effort, is leading his last reserves into the fray and will fight shoulder to shoulder with his men (**2**). By temperament a soldier, Caesar's bravery – unlike the final outcome on this day – is not in doubt. Everything now hinges on which side can keep going the longest and whose hand weapons will prove the most effective. However, there is also the vital question of whether any forces so far uncommitted can wrest back the advantage for their side. Here, perhaps, Caesar appears to have the edge. In the background and to the rear of the battling Gauls, we can catch a glimpse of the arriving Germanic horsemen, who are about to have an impressive impact (**3**).

presumably starving and exposed (*BG* 7.78.5). He gives no hint of their eventual fate (the tribe disappear from the record after Caesar). As always, Caesar's *commentarii* are concise and to the point.

It is easy to view Caesar's decision as an act of calculated callousness, yet Cassius Dio (*HR* 40.40.3) states that he refused to admit them because he was short of supplies; moreover Caesar expected them to be received back into the *oppidum*, thus increasing the pressure on Alesia. Those left inside, the ones deemed useful, were already weakened by the hardships of the siege, by the sleepless nights and the fatigue of weeks of continuous fighting. Brought to their knees, the defenders finally admitted defeat. Vercingetorix gave himself to his subordinates to kill him or hand him over to the Romans. Alesia surrendered the next day. According to Plutarch, it was 'thought to be impregnable by reason of the great size of its walls and the number of their defenders'. This did not stop Caesar from besieging it, however, and 'his peril at Alesia was famous, since it produced more deeds of skill and daring than any other of his struggles' (*Caes.* 27.1, 3). Gergovia had been paid for.

Alesia was to be the last significant Gallic resistance to the will of Rome. It involved virtually every Gaulish tribe, including the normally pro-Roman Aedui, who had maintained friendly relations with Rome since as far back as 122 BC; Aeduan warriors had served as auxiliaries, particularly as horsemen, in Roman armies. The Gauls had now been totally defeated, and there were enough captives for each legionary to be awarded one to sell as a slave; each officer received several. As the captives were led away, one can imagine a second army following in their wake for trade; horse dealers, cloth sellers, ironsmiths, jewellers, soothsayers, actors, musicians, jugglers, panders and bawds, prostitutes and others hoping to make profit from a change of fortunes. For even the common Roman soldiers were now rich; as for the legates, they must have felt like kings.

'Le Gaulois Mourant' (Saint-Germain-en-Laye, Musée d'archéologie nationale), bronze Gallo-Roman statuette *appliqué* found in 1906 beneath the forum of Alesia. Of Pergamene inspiration, it was manufactured sometime in the 2nd century AD by a local bronze worker. Caesar gives no casualty figures for Alesia, but he does use phrases such as 'massive slaughter' and 'many of the enemy were taken and killed', and does say that the prisoners went to his men 'one apiece' (*BG* 7.88.3, 7, 89.5). In no man's land, there lay the corpses of the Mandubii. The victory had come at a terrible cost in human life. (© Bridgeman Art Library)

AFTERMATH

Battles are singular moments in history, productive of strange events. Much may depend upon a small detail, the effects of a detail may be victory, and the effects of victory may be long lasting. Alesia was such, for in a very real sense it symbolized the extinction of Gaulish liberty. Rebellions would come and go, but never again would a Gaulish warlord independent of Rome hold sway over the tribes of Gaul. To gain liberty, Vercingetorix, a strong and popular leader, had hazarded everything at Alesia, and lost.

Never one to abide a rival in the glory game, Caesar had marked Vercingetorix down for death. Taken in chains to Rome, the Gaul would languish in a subterranean hole for the next six years before being publicly displayed at Caesar's unprecedented quadruple triumph in September 46 BC. Caesar did not exercise his famous clemency in the case of his greatest enemy. After the celebrations, Vercingetorix was ritually garrotted (*HR* 43.19.3). It was a full six years after Alesia, and no more than 18 months before the Caesar's own fateful Ides of March.

People continued to live in the *oppidum* of Alesia long after Vercingetorix had been defeated and dragged off in chains. Eventually, a Gallo-Roman town prospered on the site, thanks primarily to the bronze workers who settled and worked there. At its peak the town's population numbered thousands, but it was eventually abandoned in the 5th century AD. Here we see two of the large furnaces for mass-producing metal objects. Positioned in a courtyard, they each consist of a large limestone slab supported on upright blocks; a fire would have been lit under each of the slabs. (© Esther Carré)

War may bring victories, but only politics can assure lasting conquests. As Napoleon once said, with understandable hyperbole, 'To conquer is nothing. One must profit from one's success.' Caesar's spectacular victory at Alesia no doubt enhanced his political reputation, eventually leading to his crossing of the Rubicon in 49 BC. Yet it also established Roman authority in Gaul for the ensuing five centuries. Gaul had been most brutally used by Caesar. Now, the Gauls, who had suffered every hardship and atrocity, had to choose whether to continue to rebel and suffer these again, or submit tamely. The exhausted people of Gaul were slowly brought under firm Roman control over the next four decades. This period was not entirely without its problems, and sporadic local revolts are recorded.

These difficulties apart, under Augustus the romanization of Gaul continued apace. Around 27 BC Gallia Comata was divided into three, roughly along the ethnic boundaries suggested earlier by Caesar (Aquitania, Gallia Belgica and Gallia Lugdunensis), while the 'fourth Gaul', the original province of Gallia Transalpina, now became Gallia Narbonensis. Collectively these provinces were to prove to be one of Rome's most profitable acquisitions, not only as an important agricultural region, producing grain and wine, but with perhaps thrice the population of Italy, supplying valuable manpower for the Principate army too. Although the Gauls may have been hardy, wild and difficult to tame, they made excellent soldiers under strict military discipline. By the end of Nero's principate, nearly 40 per cent of the legionaries serving in the Rhine legions were recruited from Gallia Narbonensis (Forni 1953: 157–212).

The colossal statue of an idealized Vercingetorix erected on the summit of Mont-Auxois (27 August 1865) by order of Napoleon III (1808–73) and paid for by him out of his own pocket. The five-tonne statue, made of sheet copper, stands 6.6m high, but easily tops 13m with its stone socle. The sculptor, Aimé Millet (1819–91), modelled the hero's head on the emperor of the French. Caesar (wilfully) mentions nothing about the nature or appearance of Vercingetorix, though they did meet in person on at least two occasions. The statue is full of anachronisms: the pearl necklace is utter fancy; the breastplate, helmet, sword and strips of cloth wrapped round the braes are all borrowed from other historical periods. The socle, which was designed by the architect Eugène Viollet-le-Duc (1814–79), bears the engraved inscription: 'La Gaule unie formant une seule nation animée d'un même esprit peut défier l'Univers. (César, *De Bello Gallico* VII, 29) Napoléon III à Vercingétorix'. (© Esther Carré)

COUNTING THE COST

It can be argued that Alexander the Great's direct military successor was Pompey, glorious from victories in all quarters of the world, not Caesar, destroyer of Gaul. Yet the Gallic campaigns were to Caesar a school of war, an arena in which he could learn his trade and his army could gain discipline and toughness. At the end of his long tenure in Gaul, Caesar was a cool and

Terracotta bust of Colonel Baron Eugène Georges Henri Céleste Stoffel (1821–1907) aged 86 (MuséoParc Alésia). In 1861 Napoleon III sponsored an expedition, led by the distinguished soldier and scholar Stoffel, to discover and excavate the camps and battlefields of the Gallic wars. The emperor would organize, and himself contribute with self-justificatory intentions, the magisterial *Historie de Jules César* (1865–66), to be completed at a later date by Stoffel. The son of a Swiss baron – the title became hereditary by order of Louis XVIII – who had served the first Napoleon at Waterloo, Stoffel himself had seen 'the elephant' at Magenta and Solférino (4 and 24 June 1859). His uncle, Colonel Baron Christophe Antoine Jacob Stoffel, was the first to command the French Foreign Legion on its creation in 1831. (© Esther Carré)

daring commander of a highly efficient and fanatically loyal army.

Caesar's initial conquest of Gaul had been deceptively simple. However, many of the Gaulish tribes did not remain docile for long, and their uprisings (alternating with Roman reprisals) soon assumed the aspect of a vicious circle. The Gallic campaigns ended with the fall of Uxellodunum in 51 BC, and the price paid by the Gauls was both terrible and enormous. One example is provided by the inhabitants of the *oppidum*, who had their hands cut off on Caesar's orders.

Caesar and his legions had been actively campaigning in Gaul for eight years, each season slaughtering large numbers of people and enslaving tens of thousands of others. In many of the campaigns whole landscapes were torched. The eighth *commentarius*, written by Aulus Hirtius after Caesar's death, ends with the words, 'Gaul was exhausted by so many defeats. Caesar was able to keep it peaceful by making the terms of subjection more tolerable' (*BG* 8.49).

Gaul must indeed have been 'exhausted' if, in Plutarch's estimation, Caesar 'had taken by storm more than 800 cities, subdued 300 nations, and of the three million men, who made up the total of those with whom at different times he fought pitched battles with, he had killed one million of them in hand-to-hand fighting and took as many more prisoners' (*Caes.* 15.3). During the eight years of hard campaigning some two million Gaulish males had been lost out of a population of an estimated six or seven million – a devastating proportion. Whatever their accuracy, and the population figure itself is purely conjectural, these figures reflect a perception among Caesar's contemporaries that this war against the Gauls had been something exceptional, at once terrible and splendid beyond compare. They also show Caesar's disregard for human life.

The conquest of Gaul must have looked quite different from the Gaulish side. As the Gauls had found out to their cost, Rome did not play well with others and their very existence was sometimes the only trigger necessary. It is certainly possible that Caesar pursued a deliberate policy of extermination, *pour encourager les Gaulois*; he was perfectly capable of it. In the frank language of a predator, he boasted of having killed one million Gauls. In modern terminology, this would be called ethnic cleansing, or genocide. The word itself was first coined in 1944 by the Polish lawyer Raphael Lemkim (1900–59) who constructed the noun by combining the rooted words *génos* (Greek: family, kindred, tribe, race) and *caedês* (Latin: a killing, slaughter, murder, massacre). Caesar was certainly not the first to conduct deliberate extermination of one people or nation by another. Examples from the Classical past, and ones which Caesar would have been surely familiar with, are that of Melos by Athens, Thebes by Alexander the Great and Carthage by Rome. Looking further back, Agamemnon's tirade to his brother Menelaos in Homer's *Iliad* is similarly illustrative: 'Transgressors will pay the price, a tremendous price, with their own heads, their wives and all their children. Yes, for in my heart and soul I know this well: the day will come when sacred Troy must die, Priam must die and all his people with him, Priam who hurls the strong ash spear!' (lines 186–91 Fagels). Just a few years before his birth, Caesar's uncle Marius had destroyed the Cimbri and the Teutones. Some scholars of antiquity have preferred to call these atrocities 'gendercide' rather than genocide; in the former, every man capable of bearing arms were deliberately killed and women and children (especially girls) were enslaved.

From a modern, humanistic perspective, the war in Gaul was an unjust and dirty one. What are primly termed Caesar's 'excesses' in Gaul are, in plain language, his atrocities. Nevertheless, Caesar's historical enterprise was clearly deemed valid in its own day. Yet even Caesar's Roman biographer Suetonius did not accept his justification for the conquest of Gaul. According to him, Caesar actually went about picking quarrels with neighbours, even allies, of Rome on the flimsiest of pretexts. Suetonius (*DI* 24.3, 47) actually implies that Caesar was really after riches, and even his visits to Britannia were motivated by his greed for pearls. Similarly, Tacitus says (*Agricola* 13.2) Caesar had merely pointed the way to Britannia, not acquired it, while in a more general denouncement, Seneca (*Epistulae* 95.37) condemns Caesar for his zealous pursuit of false glory. Coming from a fellow Stoic, his verbal blast throws an unpleasant light on Caesar's character.

In the end, Gaul was pacified and Caesar had the credit of adding three new provinces to the empire. Yet, as Seneca rightly said, Caesar's ruling passion was ambition. Although a laudable passion when guided by reason, possessed in the extreme and under no control it proves destructive – as it did, eventually, to Caesar himself.

VERCINGETORIX'S LEGACY

Despite an image that inextricably binds Vercingetorix with Caesar, it was his armed rebellion that provided his most fulfilling moments. Paradoxically, however, before the dawn of the 19th century, the most celebrated Gaul was not Vercingetorix but Brennos, the sacker of Rome in 390 BC. Although a shadowy figure in history, he must have been dreadfully real to the inhabitants of that city.

An exquisite silver *skyphos* (drinking vessel), decorated with bacciferous branches of myrtle (a tree sacred to Venus, ancestress-deity of the Iulii) and bearing three graffiti engraved on its foot (MuséoParc Alésia). It was discovered by Claude Gros 'Lapipe' in the outer ditch of the circumvallation crossing the Plaine des Laumes. Some believe it was planted there by Stoffel, others suggest it belonged to one of Caesar's legates or even to Caesar himself. Drinking cups in silver were highly prized possessions for affluent Romans, and from 100 BC onwards the *skyphos* became their most popular luxury vessel. (© Esther Carré)

A selection of Roman lead sling bullets (Saint-Germain-en-Laye, Musée d'archéologie nationale). Archaeological evidence, in the form of a wide variety of artefacts collected over a period of more than a century, provides objective proof that Alesia was located on the site of what is now the village of Alise-Sainte-Reine. The writer finds compelling evidence in the form of two lead sling bullets, each bearing the name of T. LABI, which can be none other than Caesar's lieutenant and right-hand man, Titus Labienus. The bullets were recovered from the site of Camp C. One other identical example has been recovered from Sens, ancient Agedincum, which served as Labienus' base camp during his summer campaign against the Parisii and the Senones. (© Esther Carré)

An Avernian gold stater (Saint-Germain-en-Laye, Musée d'archéologie nationale, inv. n° 45) bearing the legend (VERCI) NGETORIXS. Twenty-seven coins survive bearing the name either VERCINGETORIXS or VERCINGETORIXIS, 25 in gold (staters) from what was the territory of the Arverni, and two in bronze from the site of Alesia itself, where a total of 731 Celtic coins have been recovered. Though it would be fitting to see the bust as a portrait of our young Gaulish hero, in all probability it is of Apollo, a god of light and of sun as well as healing, whose Celtic name was Belenos ('bright, brilliant'). Of considerable value, it is better to see these staters as items of wealth circulating within patterns of gift exchange rather than money used for commercial exchange. (Siren-Com)

Vercingetorix, without doubt, was Caesar's greatest Gaulish foe, and after 19 centuries of historical absence he made a dramatic comeback, especially in France's national myth as a symbol of Gallic resistance to the threat of a full-scale invasion. Under the monarchy, the history of France and of the monarchy were seen as identical, going back to the first Frankish kings; this left little room for the Gauls. The 1789 Revolution and the empire changed all that. Vercingetorix was not 'French' at all, no more than Boudica was 'British', but these two Celtic warlords were both resurrected as the heroic embodiments of national identity. In Vercingetorix's case, though he was the clear loser at Alesia, he had forged the first ever pan-Gaulish alliance of tribes.

For the French historian and philologist Camille Jullian (1859–1933), Vercingetorix had the stature of a Hannibal or a Mithridates (2012: chap. 21, p. 1). Moreover, the young Arvernian prince has become a romantic national icon to various groups within France. During World War II, he symbolized the heroic struggle of *la Résistance* against Hitler, the arch-imperial aggressor, while at the same time served (alongside his martyrize successor, Jeanne d'Arc) as a loyal patriot of the Vichy regime.

Vercingetorix has not escaped historical criticism, of course. The influential writer Montaigne (*Essais* 2.34, 'Observation sur les moyens de faire la guerre de Jules César') was not the last Frenchman to question his wisdom in seeking refuge in Alesia. This choice, Montaigne writes, was what allowed Caesar to extinguish the flames of Gallic rebellion.

THE BATTLEFIELD TODAY

Battlefields often fall under the shadow of archaeological threat, falling prey to the ravages of modern planning. For Alesia aficionados, however, the MuséoParc Alésia, built beneath the village of Alise-Sainte-Reine and inaugurated on 26 March 2012, is a real must and recommended for all ages.

Chef Gaulois (MuséoParc Alésia), a Gaulish horseman proudly cast in bronze in 1864 by the sculptor Emmanuel Frémiet (1824–1910). This statuette, commissioned by Napoleon III, nicely reflects a newfound nationalistic pride in the Gallic roots of French culture (in 1874 Frémiet was to sculpt the gilded bronze equestrian statue of Jeanne d'Arc at the Place des Pyramides, Paris). Over the centuries, French historians, artists, pundits and politicians have created an emphatically misleading view of the Gauls and Vercingetorix that has nevertheless become firmly entrenched in the collective imagination of modern France. (© Esther Carré)

Le Milliaire d'Alésia, set up on Mont-Auxois 13 June 1993 to commemorate the centenary of the Lycée Carnot, Dijon. Named after the famous 'Organiser of Victory', this was the secondary school where the American author Henry Miller (1891–1980) once spent a very miserable winter (1932/33) as an exchange professor of English, which he unsparingly recounts in *Tropic of Cancer* (1934). The milestone itself stands beside the Roman road linking Alesia with Sombernon, and the 120km trail Bibracte–Alésia. The latter route was brought to wider public attention in 2010 when nine members of the French re-enactment group Légion VIII Augusta hiked the trail in full marching order. The following year they repeated their *marche expérimental* with a couple of mules. (© Esther Carré)

Its Interpretation Centre was designed by Bernard Tschumi, the architect who also designed the Acropolis Museum in Athens. With the aid of scenic displays, detailed reconstructions, original artefacts, facsimiles and film, it provides a good overview of the siege. From the terrace on top of this cylindrical building a panoramic 360° view takes in Mont-Auxois and the surrounding valleys and hills.

A dig at the western end of Mont-Auxois in 1839 brought to light an inscription in the Gaulish language that names ALISIIA (*CIL* xiii 2880), and the significance of Alesia from then on in stoking nationalist sentiments can scarcely be exaggerated. Napoleon III – a passionate history buff and an ardent admirer of Caesar (unlike his uncle, he tended to gloss over the conqueror's atrocities) – was the first to show determined interest. Under his overall guidance, the first excavations between 1861 and 1865, directed for three years by Colonel Baron Stoffel, settled the identification of the site, and related Caesar's account to the details of local topography.

Admittedly, there are problems marrying Caesar's account with the site at Alise-Sainte-Reine, of which more below. Suffice to say at this point that his siege ring around Mont-Auxois was not as extensive or as complete as he claimed. As expected, the contravallation was located on low ground, following the water barriers where possible. The circumvallation, in contrast, ran mainly along the crests of the surrounding hills and linked together a total of eight (or seven) camps (unlike the *castella*, Caesar does not specify the number of *castra*), all of which have been identified by excavation. Three of the smaller *castella* were pinpointed and the sites of the other 20 estimated (to date, a further two have been confirmed). An extraordinary deposit of human, horse and mule bones, coins (datable to 52 BC or earlier) and Roman and Gaulish weaponry was recovered from the ditches below Mont-Réa on the north-west side of Alesia, the scene of some of the heaviest fighting (some have argued that this wealth of finds is all too convenient). The weapon finds include *pilum* shafts, boltheads for *scorpiones*, arrowheads, Gaulish slashing swords and even iron conical bosses from Germanic shields. It is pertinent to note here that the recovered Roman weapons are predominately of the throwing or firing variety. Certain authorities believe that lost *gladii* and *pugiones* (bar one dagger) were recovered after the battle.

ALESIA ALTERNATIVES

What the French call '*la querelle d'Alésia*' concerns itself with the precise location of Alesia. The debate opened in 1855 with the candidature of Alaise, in the *département* of Doubs. Suffice to say there still exists a lively, at times vitriolic, debate concerning the actual location of Alesia. The list of potential candidates is long, some of which are listed below, with their *département* in brackets:

Arles (Gard)
Alièze (Jura)
Aloise (Saône-et-Loire)
Conliège (Jura)
Guillon (Yonne)
Izernore (Ain)
Novalaise (Savoie)
Rougemont (Doubs)
Salins-les-Bains (Jura)
Syam-Cornu-Chaux-des-Crotenay (Jura)

It is interesting to note that many of the alternative sites are situated in Franche-Comté, east of the Saône (ancient Arar). This has been prompted by the text of Cassius Dio (*HR* 40.39.1), who implies that Alesia was in the territory of the Sequani, an area roughly coincident with the *département* of Jura. Caesar is certainly aware of the Saône, for he says of this river that it 'flows through the lands of the Aedui and Sequani into the Rhodanus (Rhône) so very slowly that it is impossible to tell just by looking in which direction it is flowing' (*BG* 1.12.1). He is also quite sure about Alesia being 'an *oppidum* of the Mandubii' (*BG* 7.68.1). However, we must not lose sight of the fact that Caesar's *commentarii* are a work of rhetoric and propaganda whose geographical detail may not be any more detailed or precise than was needed to give a general picture to his audience in Rome.

Despite the continued geographical controversy, research undertaken in 1905, and accelerated since the launch of the Franco-German campaign of surveys (including aerial photography) and excavations opened in 1991, have revealed more of the Roman siegeworks around Mont-Auxois. Such objective evidence provides further confirmation of Caesar's account.

A PARALLEL IN HISTORY

An episode from a more recent war provides an interesting parallel to Caesar's fortunes at Alesia. Henry V is the golden boy of 15th-century English history. Tough, decisive, athletic, active, devout, and above all undefeated, he is famously remembered as the victor at Agincourt. Few, however, recall his fortunes as the besieger of Rouen (1418–19) during the Hundred Years War.

Henry waited patiently for six months before Rouen, and his lines of investment are interesting to compare with Caesar's round Alesia. He had 'large trenches excavated between his tents and the walls, a crossbow-shot from the latter, which soon enveloped the town with a continuous contravallation [*contrevallation*]. The earth thrown to the inner side of the ditch formed a parapet, which was made to bristle with spikes. In front of this *vallum*, to stop the enemy's horse, several rows of pointed stakes were planted. Between the posts, deeply sunken covered ways gave secure communication from corps to corps. Places of arms at intervals, and barracks made with logs and young trees interlaced and covered with sods, formed fresh towns as it were round the town' (Puiseux 1867: 97–8). He threw a bridge over the Seine, about 4km above the town, and as the cold hand of winter tightened its grip his army threw up a line of circumvallation round his camps, to guard against any attempt at relief. It was like the line of contravallation in its general character, flanked at intervals by towers, and lightly garnished with cannon and *ballistae*.

By December 1418 the population of Rouen were dining on cats, dogs, horseflesh and even rats and mice. In an attempt to reduce the demands on their ever declining food stocks, the town betters expelled more than 12,000 of the poorest folk, the so-called *bouches inutiles* ('useless mouths'). Henry, just as Caesar had done at Alesia, would not allow these starving, ejected people to pass through his siege lines (though the king did allow two priests to feed them on Christmas Day). Rouen surrendered to Henry on 20 January 1419.

GLOSSARY AND ABBREVIATIONS

GLOSSARY

agger	earthen ramp
ballista/ballistae	stone-throwing artillery
caliga/caligae	hob-nailed boot
castellum/castella	redoubt or fort
castrum/castra	camp or fortress
cervus/cervi	'stag'; cheval de frise
cippi	'gravestones'; bulwark of sharpened stakes
clavicula/claviculae	'little key'; curved extension of rampart protecting gateway
cuniculi aperti	protective passageways formed of *vineae*
dolabra/dolabrae	pickaxe
gladius/gladii	sword carried by legionaries
legatus/legati	legate
lilia	'lilies'; pitfalls containing sharpened, smooth stakes
lorica	breastwork
lorica hamata	ring mail armour
mille passus/milia passuum	'one-thousand paces' – Roman mile = 1.478km
murus gallicus	walls constructed in the Gaulish style
musculi	'sheds'
oppidum/oppida	Gaulish town
pes/pedes	Roman foot = 296mm
pilum/pila	principal throwing weapon of legionaries
praetorium	command tent
primi ordines	'front rankers'; six centurions of first cohort
pugio/pugiones	dagger carried by legionaries
scorpio/scorpiones	'scorpion'; light, bolt-shooting catapult
scutum/scuta	shield carried by legionaries
stimuli	'spurs'; barbed iron spikes embedded in short wooden stakes
titulus/tituli	short mound with ditch forward of gateway
tormenta	artillery
vinea/vineae	shed, mantlet
vitis	vine stick

ABBREVIATIONS

Belo.	Philon of Byzantium, *Belopeika*
BC	Caesar, *Bellum civile*
BG	Caesar, *Commentarii de Bello Gallico*
Caes.	Plutarch, *Caesar*
Cras.	Plutarch, *Crassus*
CIL	T. Mommsen *et al.*, *Corpus Inscriptionum Latinarum* (Berlin, 1862 onwards)
DA	Vitruvius, *De architectura*
DH	Dionysius of Halikarnassos
DI	Suetonius, *Divus Iulius*
DS	Diodorus Siculus
Att.	Cicero, *Epistulae ad Atticum*
Fam.	Cicero, *Epistulae ad familiares*
Epit.	Florus, *Epitomae Historiae Romanae*
Geo.	Strabo, *Geographica*
HN	Pliny, *Historia Naturalis*
HR	Cassius Dio, *Historia Romanae*
Vat.	Cicero, *In Vatinium*

BIBLIOGRAPHY

Abranson, E., *Roman Legionaries at the Time of Julius Caesar*, Macdonald: London, 1979

Adcock, F. E., *Caesar as a Man of Letters*, Cambridge University Press: Cambridge, 1956

Allen, S., *Celtic Warrior, 300 BC – AD 100*, Osprey Publishing (Warrior 30): Oxford, 2001

Balsdon, J. P. V. D., *Julius Caesar: A Political Biography*, Athenaeum: New York, 1967

Barruol, G., 'La statue du guerrier de Vachères (Alpes-de-Haute-Provence)', *Revue archéologique de Narbonnaise* 29 (1996), pp. 1–12

Beard, M. and Crawford, M. H., *Rome in the Late Republic: Problems and Interpretations*, Duckworth: London, 1999 (2nd ed.)

Blake Tyrrel, W., *Biography of Titus Labienus, Caesar's Lieutenant in Gaul*, University of Washington thesis, 1970

Blois, L. de, *The Roman Army and Politics in the First Century before Christ*, J.C. Gieben: Amsterdam, 1987

Bradford, E., *Julius Caesar: The Pursuit of Power*, Hamish Hamilton: London, 1984

Brown, R. D., 'Two Caesarian battle descriptions: a study in contrast', *Classical Journal* 94 (1999), pp. 329–57

Brunaux, J.-L., *Les Gaulois, les Fiers Ennemis de Rome*, Éditions Gremese: Paris, 2011

Campbell, D. B., *Greek and Roman Siege Machinery, 399 BC – AD 363*, Osprey Publishing (New Vanguard 78): Oxford, 2003

——, *Siege Warfare in the Roman World, 146 BC – AD 378*, Osprey Publishing (Elite 126): Oxford, 2005

Cascarino, G., *L'Esercito Romano: Armamento e Organizzazione. Vol. I: dalle Origini alla Fine della Republica*, Il Cerchio Iniziative Editoriali: Rimini, 2007

Cawthorne, N., *Julius Caesar*, Haus Publishing: London, 2005

Cunliffe, B. W., *Facing the Ocean: The Atlantic and its Peoples, 8000 BC – AD 1500*, Oxford University Press: Oxford, 2001

——, *The Celts: A Very Short Introduction*, Oxford University Press: Oxford, 2003

Dodge, T. A., *The Great Captains*, Strong Oak Press: Stevenage, 1889 (reprinted 2002)

Fields, N., *The Roman Army of the Civil Wars, 90–30 BC*, Osprey Publishing (Battle Orders 34): Oxford, 2008

——, *Warlords of Republican Rome: Caesar versus Pompey*, Pen & Sword: Barnsley, 2008

——, *Julius Caesar*, Osprey Publishing (Command 4): Oxford, 2010

——, *Pompey*, Osprey Publishing (Command 23): Oxford, 2012

Forni, G., *Il Reclutamento delle Legioni da Augusto a Diocleziano*, Università di Pavia: Milan and Rome, 1953

Fuller, J. F. C., *Julius Caesar: Man, Soldier and Tyrant*, Wordsworth Editions: Ware, 1965 (reprinted 1998)

Gelzer, M. (trans. P. Needham), *Caesar: Politician and Statesman*, Harvard University Press: Cambridge, MA, 1968 (reprinted 1985)

Gilbert, F., *Le Soldat Romain, à la Fin de la République et sous le Haute-Empire*, Éditions Errance: Paris, 2004

Gilliver, K., *Caesar's Gallic Wars, 58–50 BC*, Osprey Publishing (Essential Histories 43): Oxford, 2002

Goguey, R., Le Piolot-Ville, M., Sartiaux, F. and Violota, A., *Alésia Vu du Ciel*, Éditions SEM: Alésia, 2008

Goldsworthy, A. K., *The Roman Army at War, 100 BC – AD 200*, Clarendon Press: Oxford, 1996 (reprinted 1998)

——, *In the Name of Rome: The Men Who Won the Roman Empire*, Phoenix: London, 2003 (reprinted 2004)

Goudineau, C., *César et la Gaule*, Éditions Errance: Paris, 1990

——, *Le dossier Vercingétorix*, Éditions Actes Sud/Errance: Arles, 2001

Grant, M., *Julius Caesar*, Weidenfeld & Nicolson: London, 1979

Halleck, H. W., *Elements of Military Art and Science*, D. Appleton & Co.: New York, 1862 (3rd ed.)

Harmand, M. J., *Une Campagne Césarienne, Alésia*, A. et J. Picard et Cie: Paris, 1967

——, *L'Armée et le Soldat à Rome, de 107 à 50 avant Notre Ère*, A. et J. Picard et Cie: Paris, 1969

——, *Vercingétorix*, Fayard: Paris, 1984

Hobley, B., 'An experimental reconstruction of a Roman military turf rampart', *Roman Frontier Studies, 1967: The Proceedings of the Seventh International Congress Held at Tel Aviv* (1971), pp. 21–33

Jullian, C., *Vercingétorix*, Éditions Tallandier: Paris, 1901 (reprinted 2012)

Keegan, J., *The Mask of Command*, Jonathan Cape: London, 1987

Keppie, L. J. F., *The Making of the Roman Army*, Routledge: London, 1984 (reprinted 1998)

——, 'A centurion of *legio Martia* at Padova?', *Journal of Roman Military Equipment Studies* 2 (1991), pp. 115–21

Kromayer, J. and Veith, G., *Heerwesen und Kriegführung der Griechen und Römer*, C. H. Beck: München, 1928

——, *Schlachtenatlas zur antiken Kriegsgeschichte*, 5th installment: Greek II, 6 & 7; Roman III, 15–18, Wagner & Debes: Leipzig, 1929

Le Bohec, Y., 'Vercingétorix', *Rivista Storica dell'Antichità* 28 (1998), pp. 85–120

Le Gall, J., *Alésia: Archéologie et Histoire*, Éditions Errance: Paris, 1990 (3rd ed.)

——, *La bataille d'Alésia*, Publications de la Sorbonne: Paris, 1999

Lloyd, E. M., *Vauban, Montalembert, Carnot: Engineer Studies*, Chapman & Hall: London, 1887

Martin, P.-M., *Vercingétorix: Le Politique, le Stratège*, Perrin: Paris, 2009 (2nd ed.)

Mathieu, F., *Le Guerrier Gaulois du Hallstatt à la Conquête Romaine*, Éditions Errance: Paris, 2007

——, *Le guerrier gaulois*, Éditions Errance: Paris, 2008

Meier, C. (trans. D. McLintock), *Caesar*, Harper Collins: London, 1995

Morgan, L., '*Levi quidem de re…* Julius Caesar as tyrant and pedant', *Journal of Roman Studies* 87 (1997), pp. 23–40

Napoléon III, *Historie de Jules César – Tome Deuxième, Guerre des Gaules*, Henri Plon: Paris, 1866

Ó hÓgáin, D., *The Celts: A History*, The Collins Press: Cork, 2002

Parker, H. M. D., *The Roman Legions*, Heffer & Sons: Cambridge, 1928 (reprinted 1958)

Peddie, J., *The Roman War Machine*, Sutton: Stroud, 1994

Pucci, G., 'Caesar the Foe: Roman Conquest and National Resistance in French Popular Culture', in M. Wyke (ed.) *Julius Caesar in Western Culture*, Blackwell: Oxford, 2006, pp. 190–201

Puiseux, M. L., *Siege et Prise de Rouen par les Anglais, 1418–1419*, E. Le Gost-Clérisse: Caen, 1867

Rambaud, M., *L'Art de la Déformation Historique dans les Commentaires de César*, Les Belles Lettres: Paris, 1966 (2nd ed.)

Reddé, M. (ed.), *L'Armée Romaine en Gaule*, Éditions Errance: Paris, 1996

Reddé, M. and von Schnurbein, S. (eds.), *Alésia at la Bataille du Teutoburg: un Parallèle Critique des Sources*, Jan Thorbecke Verlag: Ostfildern, 2008

Reddé, M., *Alésia: l'Archéologie Face à l'Imaginaire*, Éditions Errance: Paris, 2012 (2nd ed.)

Rice Holmes, T., *Caesar's Conquest of Gaul: A Historical Narrative*, Clarendon Press: Oxford, 1911 (2nd ed.)

Ritchie, W. F. and Ritchie, J. N. G., *Celtic Warriors*, Shire (Shire Archaeology 41): Princes Risborough, 1985

Ross, A., *The Pagan Celts*, John Jones: Ruthin, 1970 (reprinted 1998)

Sabin, P., 'The face of Roman battle', *Journal of Roman Studies* 90 (2000), pp. 1–17

Shirley, E. A. M., *Building a Roman Legionary Fortress*, Tempus: Stroud, 2001

Simon, A., *Vercingétorix et l'Idéologie Française*, Imago: Paris, 1989

Smith, R. D., *Service in the post-Marian Roman Army*, Manchester University Press: Manchester, 1958

——, 'The significance of Caesar's consulship', *Phoenix* 18 (1964), pp. 303–13

Vauban, Sébastien Le Prestre de (trans. and ed. G. A. Rothrock), *A Manual on Siegecraft and Fortification*, University of Michigan Press: Ann Arbor, MI, 1968

Welch, K. and Powell, A. (eds.), *Julius Caesar as Artful Reporter: The War Commentaries as Political Instruments*, Duckworth: London, 1998

Yavetz, Z., *Julius Caesar and his Public Image*, Thames & Hudson: London, 1983

INDEX

References to images are in **bold**.